A Rhetoric of Remnants

A Rhetoric of Remnants

Idiots, Half-Wits, and
Other State-Sponsored Inventions

Zosha Stuckey

SUNY PRESS

Cover: New York State Asylum for Idiots, circa 1890.
New York State Archives, Public Domain

Published by
STATE UNIVERSITY OF NEW YORK PRESS
Albany

Printed in the United States of America

For information, contact
State University of New York Press
www.sunypress.edu

Production, Laurie Searl
Marketing, Fran Keneston

Library of Congress Cataloging-in-Publication Data

Stuckey, Zosha, 1971–
A rhetoric of remnants : idiots, half-wits, and other state-sponsored inventions / Zosha Stuckey.
pages cm
Includes bibliographical references and index.
ISBN 978-1-4384-5301-9 (hc : alk paper) 978-1-4384-5302-6 (pb : alk paper)
E-ISBN 978-1-4384-5303-3 (ebook)
1. Mental retardation facilities—United States—History. 2. Mental retardation facilities—New York (State)—History. 3. People with mental disabilities—Education—United States—History. 4. Mental retardation facilities patients—United States—History. 5. Mental retardation—United States—History. 6. Sociology of disability—United States. I. Title.
HV3006.A4S786 2014
362.3'850974766—dc23 2013043165

10 9 8 7 6 5 4 3 2 1

This book is dedicated to the Self-Advocates of Central New York, some who were institutionalized in Syracuse but now maintain authority over their own lives, and to Ken who lost his life because no one knew how to listen to someone who did not speak.

Contents

	List of Illustrations	ix
	Acknowledgments	xi
1.	Introduction: Rhetoric, Historical Recovery, and the New York State Asylum-School	1
2.	"Confusion into Order Changed": The Rhetorics That Govern(ed) Institutionalization	15
3.	In Pursuit of the Active Life: The Roots, Rhetoric, and Recursiveness of "Special" (All) Education	53
4.	In Pursuit of the Underlife of an Archive	97
5.	Conclusion: Idiocy—An Old, Worn-Out Story	127
	Notes	137
	Bibliography	145
	Index	155

Illustrations

Figure 1.1	A small group of asylum pupils, circa 1900. The New York State Archives, Public Domain	8
Figure 1.2	Asylum Pupils, circa 1900. The New York State Archives, Public Domain	9
Figure 2.1	The Asylum in its early years. The New York State Archives, Public Domain	19
Figure 3.1	By the 1890s, pupils formed an asylum orchestra. The New York State Archives, Public Domain	70
Figure 3.2	Pupils performing exercises in front of a stage, circa 1890s. The New York State Archives, Public Domain	71
Figure 3.3	Poster displayed at the 1901 World's Exhibition in Buffalo. The New York State Archives, Public Domain	76
Figure 3.4	Women ironing, circa 1890. The New York State Archives, Public Domain	85

Acknowledgments

Thanks first to my mentor, Lois Agnew, for teaching me how to be a careful researcher, writer, and scholar. I am indebted to the Composition and Cultural Rhetoric program at Syracuse University, to Eileen Schell and Chris Palmer, to the Center on Human Policy and Disability Studies at Syracuse University, and to Jay Dolmage. I thank Steven J. Taylor, Cindy Colavita, Rachel Zubal-Ruggieri, the Beyond Compliance Coordinating Committee, Liat Ben Moshe, and Carolyn Ostrander for offering support and inspiration. I am forever grateful for my cohort at Syracuse, for my mentors in my master's program at Towson University, and to Robert McCruer for introducing me to disability studies at a reading group in D.C. in 2003. To my mother, who swore she would read it, to my father who isn't here to see it, and to my siblings for their loving quips and wisecracks. And of course, to my beloved Robin who keeps me laughing through the entire thing.

CHAPTER 1

Introduction

Rhetoric, Historical Recovery, and the New York State Asylum-School

Minding the Gap

Gaps in the historical record have always intrigued me. Initially, I was lured by the fact that the progressive activist and orator Helen Keller received no audience in anthologies of rhetoric. Perhaps her exclusion was due to the fact that her speeches were delivered via verbal translations of sign language—a form of delivery quite different from traditional oration. Nevertheless, aside from Lois J. Einhorn's work on Keller's rhetoric and Davis W. Houck and Amos Kiewe's rhetorical study on Roosevelt and his disability, there is a dearth of books on rhetoric and disability. A cadre of both scholars and activists are, however, attempting to fill in these historical and also material gaps that have privileged biological and medical meanings of disability over social, cultural, political, and historical ones. This new trend understands rhetoric as more than orality and speech giving; rhetoric and disability in this sense is embodied and at times nonverbal.

An example that further epitomizes this need for inclusion is the way in which disability activists in New York City have pushed for the city's subway system to fill in the ten- to fifteen-inch-wide platform gaps that exist between some station platforms and the train.[1] According to the Americans with Disabilities Act (1991), the subway platform gap should not exceed more than three inches. Multiple people have died as a result of the oversized gaps, and while the city has begrudgingly installed retractable walkways in a few stations, people who use wheelchairs still cannot access all trains because of inconsistent elevator service. In addition to these and other modifications needed to create a more universally accessible physical environment, the disability rights movement has also attended to gaps in historical accounts. It is these gaps that most interest me here.

This book, while not about oversized subway platform gaps, oratory, or Helen Keller specifically *is* an attempt to expand how we think about participation across a broader spectrum of difference. A far cry from homogenous, the ways we engage as humans, citizens, and as communicators are diverse, and my aim in this book is to advance social, relational, silent, and embodied action as crucial elements of civic and rhetorical engagement. I construct a *rhetoric of remnants* from the archive and from our past that recognizes mainstream, verbal, and textual political participation as only one aspect of a wide range of ways to be civically engaged in the world.

Allied with the disability rights movement, new theories on disability and rhetoric (Brueggemann, Dolmage, Duffy, Dunn, Lewieki-Wilson, Price, Vidali), and studies of rhetoric and education (Cobb, Enoch, Gold, Logan, Royster), I look at the rhetoric in and around the first thirty years of the New York State Asylum for Idiots[2] (1854–1884) or what I call the "asylum-school." I piece together how language constructed the "idiot" in the nineteenth century into a seemingly real entity, how asylum educational practices (the art of becoming, bodily transformation, civic usefulness, control of the will, imitation, speaking, writing, listening) molded pupils in ways that inspire broader educational philosophy, and how study of the actual gaps and silences themselves in discourse can be fruitful. I retrieve remnants from the archives in order to construct a social history that brings presence to people with disabilities in New York State's history.

Today, the "asylum-school" is memorialized as the first public school for people considered "feeble-minded" or "idiotic."[3] The "idiot" had, for many centuries, been viewed in contrast to "rational man" as hopeless, degraded, even wicked, inhuman, and depraved.[2] Idiot, derived from the Greek *idiotes*, which referred to a private person who did not partake in the democratic process, had come to signify lack of intelligence and mental and physical abnormality. Though we now consider someone with intellectual differences *intellectually disabled*, the term *idiot* still carries much symbolic, rhetorical, and paradigmatic force.

Much of the rhetorical nature of "idiocy," and even intelligence itself, can be traced to the period when the asylum-school first opened in Syracuse in 1854. Pupils arrived at the school after long journeys from across the state with the pseudo-scientific label of "idiot." While Alfred Binet's metric intelligence scale,[4] which developed into the IQ test, was not officially used until 1905, the ways people looked, talked, and moved were measures used to determine intelligence in the mid-nineteenth century (Fletcher-Janzen,

407). I create this mid-nineteenth-century microhistory as a pivot point in which to recalibrate ways we conceive of presence and participation; I revive the so-called civically dead idiot of the nineteenth century into a significant historical force that complicates the physical and intellectual norms we so highly prize. Participation in civic endeavors does not always have to be verbal, nor does it have to be political. In minding gaps in the historical record, we can conceptualize rhetoric and participation in more inclusive ways.

Rhetoric

While some think of rhetoric as political muckraking, this book ascribes a more complex meaning to the term. Rhetoric in this book signifies symbolic and persuasive action (social, relational, silent, and embodied uses of language) that *includes* people and groups but also *excludes* them. Rhetoric is the negotiation that we engage in with each other, privately and civically, individually and collectively, silently and discursively to attempt to reconcile our multiplicitous needs relating to action and engagement in the world. Throughout the book, access, presence, and participation are my guideposts in coming to terms with how symbolic and persuasive action undergird the ability not just to take part in educational and self-guided endeavors but to have worth as a person simply because one is human. People use rhetoric to gain access to a broad array of the social, relational, material, and humanizing things they want and need. People need rhetoric to access public space, mealtime, authorized leave, mobility, healthcare, self-governance, employment, support, relationships, and community. In the Ciceronian sense,[5] rhetoric offers people a way to foster "constructive relationship[s] between individuals and their community," to achieve virtue through civic commitment, and to attain some sense of collective unity and shared understanding (Agnew, 3, 33).

In carving out space in rhetorical history for people with disabilities, I develop the understanding that civic participation must be understood in ways that acknowledge imposed constraints. So while for some citizens work as a seamstress might not qualify as the civic life Cicero thought to be rhetoric's ultimate goal, for others work as a seamstress is civically vital. By disrupting the social versus civic opposition, we are guaranteed to include rhetorical practices other than just the political, and we are charged to view citizenship and its rhetorical practices across a broader spectrum of difference. In the asylum-school, modes of civic commitments extend beyond verbal communication and beyond political deliberation since words, when they are available, are often used in the most functional and utilitarian sense. As Brenda Brueggemann and Cheryl Glenn have reiterated, our intellectual traditions are complicit in what Brueggemann calls "the audiological moment" as it valorizes spoken language and consequently pathologizes and excludes those who do not, or wish not to, speak. One example, then, of approximations of normalcy (we are all "approximately" normal, which really means there is no normal) includes the "will to speech" that Brueggemann discusses as typifying how we think about rhetoric. I concur that the speaking subject can no longer stand as the only progenitor of knowledge. Our orientation to spoken word shifts—from one camp, the question is asked: *Who speaks?* From another camp, the question is adjusted: *How have other means created access?*

I am also interested in *rhetoric* as it is enveloped in the urge to improve and transform: the rehabilitation of the famed orator Demosthenes, and his transformation from the "abnormal" to the "normal," acts as an important cultural myth.[6] Similarly, rhetoric in the asylum-school circulates through bodies as a way to showcase the marvel of progressive educational technique. Education in this instance could not function without rhetoric: both consolidate to construct the notion of "idiocy" which then compels moral, physical, social, and civic transformation. This process of transformation into a second nature is known as *phusiopoesis*. And while any educational project ideally entails such transformations, rhetoric at the asylum-school is unique because the discourses of pathology, abnormality, and deficiency are so profoundly read through the body.

The practices I discuss from the nineteenth-century asylum operate as benchmarks for how education is always deeply rhetorical and ideological in the sense that discourses move through student bodies, and education attempts to normalize them at all costs. My study demonstrates how rhetorical fitness in the form of civic participation is possible for all regardless of whether the body is able to move (or not move) and speak (or not speak) in prescribed ways. I regard rhetoric as more than speaking and writing: rhetoric is ideology that attempts to transform the subject via the body and it is the ability for that subject to establish civic and public presence even when speaking and writing are pedagogically deemphasized. In carving out space in history for people with disabilities, I develop the understanding that civic participation must be understood in ways that acknowledge imposed constraints. So while for some citizens work as a seamstress might not qualify as the civic life Cicero thought to be rhetoric's ultimate goal, for others work as a seamstress is civically vital. By disrupting the social versus civic opposition, we are guaranteed to include rhetorical practices other than just the political, and we are charged to view citizenship and its rhetorical practices across a broader spectrum of difference.

Rhetoric and Remnants

Rather than defining rhetoric as oratory or as verbal persuasion, a revised understanding values rhetorical inquiry as a complex and multilayered epistemological and methodological tool for negotiating gaps and silences in historical evidence in order to acknowledge various versions of "reality." Rhetoric, then, includes language practices, bodily performances, and symbol usages that operate within systems of power, but it also entails barely audible traces, invisible performances, and non-extant experience that have no tangible evidence left. Rhetoric is the multiplicitous use of language (utterance or enunciation) but rhetoric is also the existence of silence that—and this is crucial—must not necessarily be confused with absence.[7]

Regrettably, I can only minimally recover the actual spoken or written words of the pupils: the remnants of a forgotten past. This is due to the fact that some did not necessarily speak in the physiologic sense, and those who did speak were often only taught to write in a rudimentary manner. As I explain further in chapter 3, asylum-school curriculum only emphasized speaking when it made sense for the individual pupil and only emphasized writing that fell within common school modes of orthography, imitation, and basic letter writing home. In order to extend rhetoric beyond speaking or writing, rhetoric includes seemingly silent practices such as "escape," traces, imprints, and inscriptions of action (like the stamping of a symbol onto a page via printing methods), joining the service, digging the Erie Canal, all that hold meaning and are in fact communicative but not through the speaking or writing of the person who experienced these things. Such practices illustrate rhetorical competence because they are meaningful expressions that alter how we think of who is a fit rhetor: fitness does not necessarily manifest through the written or spoken word. Rather, rhetorical fitness comes about less through alphabetic modes and more through objects and actions.

In my study of the asylum-school, rhetoric is all of these things—a negotiation, access, and silence. Put together, study of rhetoric at the asylum-school urges us to think more deeply about how our seemingly straightforward methods for recovering evidence can themselves erase people. In their anthology, Longmore and Umansky ask, "How can one write the history of a subject if one cannot gather much evidence about it?" (6). According to historian Henri Stiker, rehabilitation as a medical science is that which tries to make disability invisible—to make it go away. He writes, "Rehabilitation marks the appearance of a culture that attempts to complete the act of identification, of making identical. This act will cause the disabled to disappear and with them all that is lacking, in order to drown them, dissolve them in the greater and single social whole" (170–71). David Mitchell and Sharon Snyder go so far as to call the erasure part of an "ideology of extinction" (*Cultural Locations*, 32).

I build upon theses ideas by using methodologies that make sense amidst a technology of erasure: historical ethnography, revisionist historiography, feminist and Afra-feminist rhetorics, and feminist disability studies. These methodologies are overlapping and complementary. What is more, my historiographic work sometimes has more to do with absence than presence. This principle of absence is abundant in the historical record of the asylum-school in general but there is even more absence in the record in terms of the voices of the nondominant groups—the pupils and their families. While more than a few thousand people passed through the asylum, only Superintendent Wilbur and his mentor Dr. Edouard Seguin are identifiable by name in photographs in the archival record from the New York State Archives in Albany, the Onondaga Historical Society, and random remnants still housed at the building site. With a few exceptions, almost everyone other than Wilbur and Seguin are anonymous. Another example of absence includes the fact that the campus that was the New York State Asylum grew in the early twentieth century to include fifty buildings and structures; yet today, not one of the original structures remains. A few years ago, the last remaining structure—a small gatehouse—was demolished in order to keep local teenagers from using it as a midday escape from high school. Multiple other asylums have been demolished and while the list is long, a few include Elgin State Hospital (1993), Danvers (2006), Worcester (2007), and Willard (1995). As large state institutions or asylums began to close down in the 1990s, those that have not been demolished have been turned into prisons or state office buildings, or have sat abandoned.

Further, when inmates died at New York State Asylum for Idiots and did not have family burial arrangements they were buried in unnamed graves in Oakwood Cemetery in Syracuse. Anonymously numbering graves was a typical practice and represents the capstone of historical erasure, as the image of a gravestone from Rome Asylum for Unteachable Idiots (est. 1898 in Central New York) shows only a number.[8] A recent find in the history of asylums in Central New York occurred when, just before Willard State Hospital was demolished, a curator from the New York State Archives found suitcases that contained the possessions (including letters) of inmates of the insane asylum. From the artifacts in the suitcases, Penney Darby and Peter Stastny reconstructed the lives of the inmates in a traveling exhibit and book entitled *The Lives They Left Behind: Suitcases from a State Hospital*. The story of my book is likewise one of absence, erasure—and, also, the ensuing struggle to gather remnants and piece together lost lives.

The archival remnants of this project are well-preserved annual reports[9] of the institution (no suitcases have been found), professional journal articles and books by educators at the asylum, pupil evaluation reports, and an endless supply of bound ledgers that list Christmas gifts received, visitors, letters received, clothes received, packages received, runaways, admittances, parole (release), as well as letters, posed photographs, text from handwriting lessons, curricular documents, inspection reports, safety procedures, other administrative documents, material produced by inmates in the print shop, and hand-sown mittens. My project weaves together these remnants from varied sources and thus develops a rhetorical history that makes something out of what was thought to be disconnected and lost. The closest thing to "case histories" included "pupil evaluation reports," which preceded extensive patient (student) case files. These reports offer minimal information in columns labeled name, age, date, residence, habits, conduct, capacity for occupation, ability to comprehend language, speak, know of colors, draw, imitate, write, read, and count.

While many records do not take me beyond the institutional voice, these difficulties serve historiographic purposes in the sense that I have attempted (at least in chapter 4) to write *about* an institution without placing the dominant voices of the institution at the forefront. This means accessing letters written by family members of inmates, uncovering agency and voice in the institutional displays and exhibits that were preserved in the archive, constructing productive labor such as the work done in the print shop as a certain type of "voice," and seeking histories through poorhouse records and census reports. When I began the project, I assumed I would have to rely heavily on medicalized sources: institutional documents and professional journal articles by "experts." I confronted what I considered obstacles that forced me to question my emphasis on these institutional sources. It was fortuitous that I stumbled upon a set of letters (*The James Thornton Correspondence*) written to the mother of a pupil. This as well as other methodological complexities I confront in the book has forced me not only to look even harder for subaltern voices, but also, in doing so, to recognize how complex asylum, pupils', and families' perspectives must have been. While I am aware throughout the book of my own position as a historian with her own particular prejudices, I attempt to be as fair and accurate as possible. I have earnestly tried to not judge the past based on my own views, especially concerning contemporary notions of disability rights and deinstitutionalization.

The Asylum-School, Its Pupils, and the Closing of the Institution

Due to the nature of what remains in the archive, most if not all of what we know about who attended the school is from pedagogical and annual reports. There is little information written from the perspectives of pupils and their families other than from a small collection of letters and artifacts that I discuss in depth in chapter 4. We do know that upon arrival at the school, the appearance and physiologic function, including language ability, of a pupil were described in detail. Pupils are said to have an "imperfect physical organization" (1st *Annual Report*, 44–45). Some are described as having an "unordinary" head or face (ibid). Some have vacant eyes while others have a wandering gaze. Some are reported as restless and others as partially immobile, and still others as entirely inert (ibid., 51). Reports read that seven walked imperfectly, three had partial paralysis, eleven had experienced convulsions, eight had excessive flow of saliva, seven were "inattentive to the calls of nature," five were irritable, some were unable to dress themselves, and only four were reported to be able to "feed themselves with propriety. . . . None of them could read or write, or count, or distinguish colors by name" (ibid., 44–45).

At its opening in Syracuse in 1854, the asylum-school was a relatively small educational and rehabilitative institution of about fifty pupils, none of whom were labeled "mad" or "insane." Insane asylums arose around the same period as "idiot asylums," but while the two types of institutions share various characteristics, they should not be confused. Moreover, that

Figure 1.1. A small group of asylum pupils, circa 1900. The New York State Archives, Public Domain.

Figure 1.2. Asylum Pupils, circa 1900. The New York State Archives, Public Domain.

the asylum-school educated only those considered to have what we today call intellectual disabilities is not entirely true. Nancy Ordover reports that Henry Goddard's 1912 IQ examinations concluded that more than 80 percent of all Jewish, Polish, Italian, Hungarian, and Russian immigrants that came through Ellis Island were feeble-minded defectives (11). I emphasize this thread that suggests that "idiocy" and "feeble-mindedness," rather than inscrutable scientific or biological truths, were rhetorical constructions influenced by hegemonic views on race, class, gender, and ability.[10]

The school was part of Horace Mann's movement for free and universal education; yet, also, it diverged from those principles in that some paid for their schooling at the asylum and some attended because they were not welcomed into mainstream schools. Mann, the progressive educator who played a central role in organizing the common school movement in Massachusetts, had visited Europe to tour schools in 1848 with Samuel Gridley Howe,[11] who was a close comrade to Hervey Backus Wilbur, the superintendent and founder of the asylum-school in Syracuse. With the support of Howe, Mann, and other prominent citizens,[12] Wilbur opened an experimental school first in Albany in 1851, which then expanded to Syracuse in 1854.

In 1855, eighty-nine students attended the asylum-school. By the 1880s, industrial education took precedence over academics (*Annual Report*, 1852–1884). By 1931, 1,437 people of all ages lived and worked at the school and at thirteen allied colonies (*Census Report*). Years later, in 1969, the first group home in the community was established in Syracuse, followed by the building of a new, smaller facility (called the Syracuse Developmental Center). In 1975, residents formed their own council inside the institution and began to organize alongside the Disability Rights, Patients' Rights, and Self-Advocacy Movements (see the Self-Advocates of Central New York and Self-Advocacy Association of New York State). With a growing number of reports of abuse and neglect, and with the nationally publicized closure in 1987 of the Willowbrook Institution in Staten Island, 144 years after it opened its doors, in 1998 the last five residents moved into group homes and independent living residences. There, people receive case management, cultural integration, and medical and educational support across a broad continuum in terms of both quantity and quality (Center on Human Policy).

This shift to more recent inclusion models came about through decades of civil rights advocacy. Following this civil rights trajectory, scholarship in the field of rhetoric emerged in the 1980s and onward that included North American revisionist histories of abolitionist, women's rights, African American, Latina/o and Native American, and gay, lesbian and transgendered rhetorics. However, as *Octalog III: The Politics of Historiography* and its critiques confirmed, this work of inclusion has not been theorized sufficiently. This book responds to these critiques by reconceptualizing rhetoric and civic engagement in more inclusive ways that are aligned with disability studies and feminism.

Disability Studies and Feminist Rhetorics

The disciplinary field of disability studies asks that critical study of disability be deployed as a natural supplement to the classic interpretive framework that includes race, class, gender, ethnicity, age, sexual orientation, religion, etc. Yet, even with a surge of recent writing about diverse communities, integrating disability into our material, ideological, and historical pursuits has not been easy or expeditious. Rather, it requires large disciplinary changes in ways of thinking that, most of all, include employing (dis)ability as a positive signifier historically, culturally, theoretically, pedagogically, and personally. We need to deploy disability not within the usual physical or intellectual deficit model, but as a complex social, rhetorical, and historical ideology.

One core ideological underpinning of disability studies is the social model of disability, which contends that rather than only a biologically determinable category, disability is at least partially socially constructed and cultural and historical. A social constructivist theory is important because it splinters biological deterministic notions that say that bodily difference warrants dissimilar treatment. For example, people who cannot use stairs often have to enter through the back door of a building. But for social constructivism, what was previously attributable to biology is now ascribed to social mechanisms. Everyone, in theory, needs to enter through the front door. That is, when we think of a nineteenth-century "asylum for idiots"—after the initial giggle dissipates[13]—we must conceive of the term *idiot* as a complex, historically situated social and rhetorical construction. James Trent, Steven J. Taylor, Douglas Biklen, and multiple others argue that in fact intellectual disability is a social construction that threatens the cultural order; it is an imagined antithesis of American success. It is, as Rosemarie Garland-Thomson calls disability, the ultimate Other against which we compare ourselves.

This all begs the question, If disability has such a strong theoretical bent, how then have there not been more histories of people with disabilities? If, as Paul Longmore and Lauri Umansky write, "[d]isability has been present, in penumbra if not in print, on virtually every page of American History" (2), why has it been so nominal? In their anthology entitled *The New Disability History: American Perspectives*, Longmore and Umansky argue that gaps in disability scholarship are not attributable to history, but rather to how history is written. And, they contend, a good deal of the historical material available on disability is composed by people with disabilities themselves. My project, however, takes this even farther to demonstrate how difficult it may indeed be to recover particular types of primary perspectives. This work is important not just to people writing about disability but also to all historians and advocates who have the desire to access primary perspectives but find that task difficult.

This book is about locating positive significations of disability on the historical map. My purpose is to include disability studies perspectives that place disabled subjects in or near the center. James C. Wilson and Cynthia Lewieki Wilson affirm the symbiotic nature of the fields of disability studies and rhetoric: "Disability studies seeks to advance the cause of the disabled and promote social change by analyzing the present social formations that contribute to maintaining walls of exclusion. Disability studies is thus a situated discourse and expresses a particular standpoint—that of the disabled. Rhetoric and composition's various methods of analysis, theories, and history can aid in this project; indeed, the goals of disability studies cannot be achieved without rhetoric" (*Embodied Rhetorics*, 9). Disability studies, as a twenty-year-old field, is highly invested in bringing about multiple ideological and societal changes: disavowal of the understanding of disability as deficit, redistribution of cultural and economic capital, and redeployment of identity as cultural and historical.

Disability studies and rhetoric need each other in the sense that while the former pushes for expanded consideration of who can be rhetorically competent, the latter puts social change into motion through discourse. Without rhetoric, the disability rights movement could not have coalesced into a cohesive group with shared values and strategic tactics, and without rhetoric, disability studies scholars could not have argued for the establishment of disciplinary auspices in the traditions of Women and Gender Studies, African American Studies, Native American Studies, etc. Rhetoric affirms for disability studies the contingent and transformative nature of "reality"; many realities exist and are constructed through the ideologies of interested groups. For example, rhetoric constitutes the symbolic interaction that allows the medical model to exist, but more importantly, rhetoric permits other "realities" such as a cultural or historical model of disability to exist as well. Rhetoric has been instrumental, however, not only in the formation of disciplinarity and the advancement of social justice, but also in the fact that people are beginning to acknowledge that the established "truths" of disability studies are themselves subjective and in need of contestation. Rhetoric confirms the continuously fraught nature of all premises, claims, and arguments as they emerge across various contexts and circumstances.

Feminist studies in particular has much in common with disability studies, which makes the alliance a natural one: both consider social constructionism, standpoint epistemology, identity, and social justice. Both are highly invested in contextualizing discussions within cultural, material, and economic circumstance. Both disability and gender signify relations of power (Garland-Thomson; Glenn; Ervelles) that beg for analysis and contestation. Both deal with an assumed biological inferiority. But rather than a biologically inferior position, disability is argued to be "a hypothetical set of guidelines for corporeal form and function arising from cultural expectations about how human beings should look and act. Although these expectations are partly founded on physiological facts about typical humans—such as having two legs with which to walk upright or having some capacity for sight or speech—their sociopolitical meanings and consequences are entirely culturally determined" (Garland-Thomson, *Extraordinary Bodies*, 7). In this book, rhetoric centers around access as it relates to embodied difference; this lens offers much in terms of expanding how we think of rhetoric.

Review of Chapters

In the following chapter, "'Confusion into Order Changed': The Rhetorics That Govern(ed) Institutionalization" (chapter 2), I begin by explaining how and why asylums came to be. This chapter is framed around the rise of institutionalization—and by proxy the rise of notions of "idiocy"—in the United States. What constituted an "idiot?" How were those determinations made? How did rhetoric facilitate not only the notion of "idiocy" but also the development and maintenance of the "idiot asylum?" I show how it was the rhetorical (syllogistic, topical, and definitional) reasoning rather than "real" biological difference that invented the "idiot." In this chapter I look at some of the tropes (metaphors and rhetorical figures) and topoi (lines of arguments) that reified the notion of "idiocy" and developed and sustained the asylum-school at Syracuse.

In chapter 3, "In Pursuit of the Active Life: The Roots, Rhetoric, and Recursiveness of 'Special'[14] (All) Education," I interpret the curriculum through concepts and practices of civic participation, the body (deportment and countenance), phusiopoesis (the art of becoming), the will, speaking, reading/writing, listening, and decorum. I piece together the actual curriculum alongside the educational ideologies as they were devised by the reformers, educators, and administrators. The philosophy of education at the asylum-school lay not only at the root of "special" education, but liberal humanist education in a broad sense has borrowed its corporeal, sensorial, experiential, and utilitarian nature. I utilize curricular and administrative documents, annual reports, and professional journals to reconstruct the curriculum and the day to day regimen as it was envisioned by those who held administrative and pedagogical power.

Chapter 4, "In Pursuit of the Underlife of an Archive,"[15] searches for the subaltern rhetorics or the perspectives of the pupils and their families. While chapter 3 discusses how education was implemented from above, this chapter will look at complex subaltern practices from below in order to reveal the presence of pupils at the asylum-school and their families in terms of how they engaged with the education offered. In this chapter, I approach the difficult historiographic work of trying to recover historical memory of those who did not necessarily speak or write; this process of retrieval, which is part and parcel of a rhetoric of silence, I argue, can inform historical methods generally. I look at the gaps in discourse in order to reconstruct what was not recorded. The historian must, at times, read between the lines. This chapter theorizes how this is done. Finally, chapter 5 concludes the project by reflecting on how this study can point us toward a more socially just and inclusive world.

Most of all, the asylum-school pupil is a monumental example of how education can (or at least attempts to) mold and rehabilitate one's being. This overhaul is remarkably ideological. Study of education at the asylum-school is an especially illuminating site due to the fact that the pupils upon admittance were deemed civically and rhetorically unfit, even *civically dead,* and identified as in need of a radical overhaul of their bodies, intellects, modes of communication, and social relations. The broad, unstable, and cross-cultural category of "people with disabilities" endures an especially interesting relationship to rhetoric, education, speaking, and writing. This project aims to demystify some of that relationship, which invariably requires new modes of inquiry and new ways of thinking. Study of the asylum-school calls into question many of our assumptions about embodied differences as they relate to pedagogy, history, and public participation. This book will, hopefully, fill in gaps by bringing us closer to understanding those complexities.

CHAPTER 2

"Confusion into Order Changed"

The Rhetorics That Govern(ed) Institutionalization

How difficult was it for many of us to be persuaded that their condition was susceptible of moral or mental improvement! With what emotions of gratitude and admiration ought we to regard the generous benefactors, who have rescued this class of beings from their degradation, bringing them from darkness to light, and awakening into new existence, the living soul which seemed to be lost in interminable night.

—Washington Hunt, ex-governor of New York,
at the opening ceremony

Wife, my prophecy is fulfilled. Idiots have been educated.

—Rev. Samuel J. May, abolitionist,
women's rights and asylum proponent

May darkness here be turned to light
—Confusion into order changed;
Souls without strength, inspired with might,
And idiots with thy children ranged.

—Hymn sung at opening ceremony

Introduction

In the mid-nineteenth century, amid vast educational reform, the "idiot" was at last afforded reclamation: with enough moral, physical, intellectual, and educational rehabilitation, he or she could be integrated into Victorian culture. "Idiots" were among the last of the "unfortunate classes" to be offered rehabilitative education: those who were prisoners, deaf,[1] blind, or insane already had institutions built for them, however flawed those institutions might have been. The "idiot" had, for many centuries, been viewed in contrast to "rational man" as hopeless, degraded, even wicked and depraved. *Idiot,* derived from the Greek *idiotes*, which referred to a private person who did not partake in the democratic process, had come to signify lack of intelligence, depravity, and mental and physical abnormality. The "idiot's" so-called depraved condition was promised to be ameliorated by new modes of philanthropy that combined Christian benevolence with progressive educational reform. Edouard Seguin's method of teaching "idiots" had developed in France and then caught the attention of Superintendent Wilbur and Samuel Howe, the man who is known to have guided the education of Helen Keller.[2] Thus, at the time of the opening of the asylum-school in Syracuse in 1854, progressive thinkers and educators were charged with convincing the public that the "idiot," too, should be provided an education.

But what constituted an "idiot?" And, how were those determinations made? How did rhetoric facilitate not only the notion of "idiocy" but also the development and maintenance of the "idiot asylum?" What does this line of inquiry reveal about ourselves in relation to rhetoric, embodied difference, and education? In this chapter, I show how it was the rhetorical (syllogistic, topical, and definitional) reasoning rather than "real" biological difference that invented the "idiot." I look at some of the tropes (metaphors and rhetorical figures) and topoi (lines of argument) that reified "idiocy" and developed and sustained the asylum-school at Syracuse. Epideictic rhetoric, or the rhetoric of praise and blame, played an especially important role here in that educators devised a continuum from pathology (blame) to reparation (praise) of the pupil; this shift, which was more linguistic than biological, was at the heart of the asylum methods examined in this study.[3]

I begin by describing the opening ceremony of the New York State Asylum for Idiots; here, the figure at work is the *asylum as noble*. Next, I describe two tropes that embody philosophies of the institution: the *asylum as school* and the *asylum as prison*. I then move to the pupils themselves. When people entered the system of the asylum-school (before and after admittance), they were signified via tropes I typologize as the *described and the counted*, the *nameless*, the *visited*, and the *displayed*. These signifiers—iconographies, if you will—were created and maintained through the complex arguments and narratives made alongside them. As signifiers, they determined how "idiocy" was acted upon, understood, and even perhaps resisted.

Prior to admission, the entirety of tropes listed above constructed the pupil as deficient, unfortunate, wretched, brutish, and also as "chosen friends," "poor creatures," and "friends of humanity." After admittance, the pupils were described as blissful, resilient, and productive. The asylum was consistently (but even more so in its first few years at Syracuse) "noble" and "majestic" while the educational philosophy and its proponents were valiant benefactors.

To further situate "idiocy" within rhetorical modes, I draw upon Michael Berube's notion of "seeing as." In *Life as We Know It: A Father, a Family, and an Exceptional Child*, Berube discusses how his son is always seen as something—as a "Mongoloid" child, as a retarded child, as a child with a developmental disability. Berube writes that this seeing his son *as* "makes for an unbearable cognitive dissonance" (xii). Asylum arguments in the nineteenth century conjure similar cognitive dissonance: pupils in the asylum-school were seen as something. This something then became an alternate, constructed reality. That is, the rhetorics of reformers and educators created constructed realities of lived experience—"idiocy" was a mother lode of constructions.

It is important to understand the social and rhetorical construction of "idiocy" because if, as Rosemarie Garland-Thomson contends in *Extraordinary Bodies*, disability is the ultimate Other against which we compare ourselves, then "idiocy" is a counterpart to notions we hold dear about ourselves. If "idiocy" is a construct, then so is intelligence. In arguing for social constructionism, I am not denying that there are embodied differences among people. Patrick McDonagh asserts in *"Idiocy": A Cultural History*:

> Certainly there are individuals so designated who need assistance in performing some—or even most—of the acts of daily life; others need occasional support services to facilitate some of the more complex elements of social life. But our interpretation of these needs has been heavily overdetermined, as have been our denials of our own similar needs in our assertions of independence and competence. Our broad cultural notions of intelligence (and its apparent lack) are laden with baggage packed with ideas and preconceptions about gender, class, ethnicity and religion, among others. Consequently, "idiocy" as a concept is nothing if not problematic, ambiguous and obscure—a shadow image (Stainton and McDonagh 2001) or, more prosaically, a social construction. (McDonagh, 5)

This chapter brings to light the ways in which we determine(d) who is intelligent and who is not and it tells us more about how rhetoric reifies those determinations.

Crucial to this chapter, and a specific rendezvous point for those who want a deeper understanding of rhetoric, is the use of figures and tropes. Many forms of knowledge in the humanities and liberal arts rely upon what are known as rhetorical figures and tropes. One example of the notion of a trope specific to disability studies may be found in its use to indicate a turn in meaning, such as disability *as* sentimental occasion or disabled person *as* overcomer. But rhetoric's use of the notion of trope extends trope (or "figure") to signify, as Jeanne Fahnestock writes in *Rhetorical Figures in Science*, "a verbal summary that epitomizes a line of reasoning" (24). A trope is arranged around a commonplace (topoi or topic) that works to familiarize us with its rhetorical functioning.

In this sense, a trope carries meaning from one "reality" to another, differently organized "reality." Behind this transference of meaning lies an extended line of argument that becomes epitomized as the trope. As Fahnestock contends, the tropes or figures are the epitomes of lines of argument. In this chapter, I am interested in how disability and embodied difference—or, in nineteenth-century terminology, how idiocy—functioned tropologically and rhetorically. The chapter, then, is framed around the rise of the first public "idiot asylum" in the United States, which is linked to the rise and codification of idiocy as a rhetorical construction. Patrick McDonagh, in his cultural history of the concept, calls idiocy "a metonymic state" (9). Idiot, half-wit, mongoloid, imbecile, moron, simpleton, dullard, fool. Bona fide know-nothings.[4] Who is the "idiot"? And, how did rhetoric underwrite the construction?

The Noble Asylum

The idea of the asylum—the "noble" asylum—arose in the United States during the early nineteenth century amid a period of widespread attempts at reform that included public education, abolitionism, women's rights, and temperance. "The asylum era," as David Rothman calls it in *Discovery of the Asylum*, "was a monument to a new ethic" (xviii); the new ethic was engulfed in ideas of pageantry and benevolent social and educational reform for all. Viewed in its day by most as an illustrious extension of the Enlightenment, the asylum, it was argued, would enable growth and improvement not only in its pupils but also in the local community and larger society, who would, supposedly, benefit from morally reformed and employable individuals. Institutionalization in asylums was considered a benevolent act that protected the weak and vulnerable from the dangers of society. Rather than wicked or debased, during this period the idiot was pitied as a victim who needed refuge from the sins of the poorhouse. The word *asylum*, from the Greek *asylon*, translates as "refuge," "sanctuary," or "retreat" and from the neutered form *asylos*, which means "inviolable." As one example of the continued heritage of the term, William Tuke's York "Retreat," an early insane asylum in Britain deemed very successful utilized such sentimental rhetoric by calling itself a "retreat."[5] The nineteenth-century asylum was seen as a happy retreat at which visitors could witness the educational and rehabilitative innovations by which those who were deemed unfit but deserving could be transformed.

By locating an asylum in Syracuse, the town and its people could claim that they acted upon a philosophy of benevolence and would be seen as part of the movement toward progressive, benevolent reform. In the burgeoning and newly incorporated (1847) town of Syracuse, an asylum promised economic resources, jobs, and cultural esteem for a town that had celebrated the opening of the Erie Canal in 1825. An asylum, it was thought, would attract visitors to the town and provide jobs to its residents. State officials

Figure 2.1. The Asylum in its early years. The New York State Archives, Public Domain.

would visit often, families would come to inquire about the school, and educators would come to observe the school's innovative techniques. By mid-century, Syracuse was a major industrial crossroads connecting New York City with the Erie Canal and the upstate municipalities it served. It was thought that a town such as Syracuse that could obtain an asylum would profit both culturally and economically from it; additionally, Syracuse had a track record as a center for progressive political movements such as abolitionism and women's rights and had operated as a way station on the Underground Railroad. The education of "idiots" and the transfer of people from poorhouses into asylums was viewed as progressive reform and welcomed into the city.

In Albany in 1851, Senator Frederick Backus, following the example of Samuel Gridley Howe's 1848 Memorial to the Legislature of Massachusetts, lobbied New York state legislators for appropriations to finance the relocation of the small experimental school for "idiots" in Albany to a larger tract of land atop a hill in Syracuse. A *New York Times* article praised Syracuse as the perfect location for an asylum: "No city in this State affords more wealth, in business and enterprise, and in social refinement than Syracuse" ("The State Idiot Asylum," May 19, 1855). Later, in 1871, the *Times* mentioned Syracuse in reference to its asylum as the perfect location:

> With what wonder and amazement [the first business owner in Syracuse—Abraham Walton] must gaze on the large and flourishing city which now covers the old cedar swamps by the lake side, on which the Onondaga Valley opens—in his day a vast dreary expanse of swamp and salt marsh, and about the most unpromising tract of real estate in which the most sanguine man could possibly be induced to speculate . . . its lofty chimneys which surely indicate an expanse of industry, salt-works, networks of railroads and canals . . . [the city is] an example of American progress, energy and enterprise. ("Our State Institutions: Syracuse Past and Present," Nov. 22, 1871)

The asylum—noble, even majestic—merited such a stately location. The asylum, it was thought, would certainly benefit the pupils who attended it, and even more, Syracuse was certain that it would see economic and manufacturing benefits come to the city via the asylum.

In the grand nineteenth-century spirit of rapid growth, economic development, and progressive reform, the New York State Asylum for Idiots officially opened in Syracuse on September 8, 1854. Several hundred citizens gathered to lay the building's cornerstone as part of what was reported to be a noble and benevolent occasion (*Daily Standard*, Sept. 9, 1854). On the day of the official opening, a Friday, many prominent men of the city and state arrived via horse-drawn carriage for the ceremony, which was to begin promptly at noon. Ladies were present, though their names are left out of the event's record, and not one of the ninety pupils who would be admitted to the school in 1855 are recorded to have attended the event. Among the men attending were Allen Monroe, the mayor of Syracuse; Elias W. Leavenworth, New York's secretary of state and the president of the Syracuse Savings Institution, the Water Works Company, and the Gas Light Company; the Honorable Washington Hunt, former governor of New York (the current governor sent his regrets due to illness); Hervey B. Wilbur, superintendent of the asylum-school; Edouard Seguin, founder of specialized physiological education for "idiots"; several Syracuse City Council members; and the abolitionist and women's rights advocate Reverend Samuel J. May.

At the cornerstone laying ceremony, interspersed between speeches by these prominent men, Reverend May adapted Christian hymns for the occasion:

> Bright source of everlasting Love, To Thee our souls we raise . . .
> Each wise design, each generous deed, Proceedeth, Lord, from Thee.
> To Thee we owe the gracious plan That bids these walls arise,
> To Thee we look in earnest prayer, To bless this enterprise.
> (4th *Annual Report*, 180–83)

May also spoke: "But there was idiocy—idiocy so appalling in its appearance, so hopeless in its nature; what could be the use of such an evil? . . . I ventured, therefore, to declare, with an emphasis enhanced . . . that the time would come when access would be found to the idiotic brain, the light of intelligence admitted into its dark chambers, and the whole race be benefited by some new discovery of the nature of mind" (4th *Annual Report*, 216). "The dark chamber" needed light. The "idiot" was "appalling," "hopeless," and yet finally there was "access" into the mind. Rather than the "idiocy" having a connection to demonism, as it arguably had for centuries, the "idiot" now had a chance to be brought out of the dark.

The ex-governor of New York went on to testify in a similar sentimental and religious tone: the "idiot" used to be "inexorable," "doomed to a state of debasement," and "too profound for amelioration" (4th *Annual Report*, 187). But now, as Dr. Seguin (founder of the main curricular method used in Europe and the United States—see chapter 3) asserted, the goal was to build "palaces for the indigent" (207). One prominent figure after another at the opening ceremony confirmed an epiphany: education could transform "poor creatures," "debased souls," and "unfortunates" into "harmonized" and contributing citizens who could perform ordinary duties, exercise their rights as individuals, and develop connections between self and community. These select terms, and longer passages as well, indicate a move to reclaim the "idiot's" place within humanity. Educational advances and the science of the mind were the vehicles that would accomplish this. The school's opening constituted the fulfillment of a sanctimonious prophecy that would, through the enlightenment of educational reform and moral treatment, lift degraded pupils out of their misery. Seguin continued: "See that stone—the token of a new alliance between humanity and a class hitherto neglected—that, ladies and gentlemen, is your pride; it is the greatest of joy of my life, for I, too, have labored for the poor idiot" (4th *Annual Report*, 208). In the language of today, these sentiments might seem harsh, overly pitying, and exaggerated; however, these educators and physicians were (and still are) seen as advocates who had advanced progressive reforms and offered certain rights to a new class of people.

To assure a glorious and lasting remembrance of the event and all the opening ceremony symbolized, the board of trustees of the school buried a twelve- by six-inch box beneath the cornerstone. It contained: (1) reports by Dr. Backus to the senate in 1846–47; (2) a report of the State Lunatic Asylum for 1846, recommending the establishment of an Asylum for Idiots; (3) the Annual Reports of the Trustees of the New York Idiot Asylum for 1852–54; (4) the Legislative Manual; (5) the Syracuse City Charter, with a list of the present officers of the city government; (6) Copies of the Syracuse daily newspapers; (7) names of the donors for the site of the institution; and (8) the program of proceedings of the day. The building's architect and carpenter were monumentalized on the cornerstone alongside the institution's trustees and its superintendent, the teacher and physician Hervey B. Wilbur. The land and the building were seemingly praised as hallowed ground; the view from the hill on which the asylum sat was "majestic." The trustees of the Syracuse Asylum for Idiots had chosen a location approximately one mile from the center of the burgeoning city. Local writers sentimentalized the Italianate building as "stand[ing] upon a lofty eminence overlooking the city of Syracuse, Onondaga Lake" (*Daily Courier*, 1858). Fruit trees grew amid fertile land, and the building had been positioned by its architects to allow a warm southern exposure for the pupils, as if the temple needed light from the Gods.

In general, the records of the dedication ceremony tell us a lot about the rhetorical strategies that operated at the opening of the school: in sanctifying the school, the building and the endeavor were exalted. The ceremonial words offered high praises to the building, the founders of the institution, and the stately work that would be performed there. This grand rhetoric of glory and beneficence typifies how most viewed the work of institutionalization, and how sentimental and epideictic rhetoric constituted a significant part of the rhetorical construction of asylums. Further, this sentimental rhetoric displaced the materiality of quotidian practices: no pupils were seen at the ceremony in their imperfect bodies. The building was revered while the living, breathing humans that would inhabit it were "chosen friends" and "poor creatures" that would now be lifted out of their degradation and animal nature.

That not one of the incoming pupils is known to have attended the cornerstone laying ceremony signifies one among many fundamental principles in the asylum model that complicate a discourse of sentimentality and nobility: that is, the pupil is both absent and present, everywhere and nowhere. The asylum had been situated in Albany from 1851 until its move to Syracuse in 1854. Fifty pupils (forty state-sponsored and ten private, or paying) were transferred from the Albany facility to the new one in Syracuse; these pupils and their families certainly could have attended the ceremony (even though reporters might never have documented it), but those considered "idiotic" would most likely not have been encouraged to be in public, and families likely would not have had money or time for travel to Syracuse (3rd *Annual Report*, 7). This apparent absence or invisibility of the pupils and their families at a celebrated administrative and political event such as the ceremony would not have been extraordinary, because their inclusion may not have been considered.

Nevertheless, the absence of the pupils is one fissure that points to the nature of the rhetorical construction of "idiocy" at that time; and although the pupils were in fact important, the identity of the building, the life of the institution, the charitable nature of its mission, and the valiant quality of the scientific and educational endeavor occupied the center of the event's oratory. The rhetoric of the opening ceremony makes a case for the asylum as a noble and benevolent endeavor, and corrals public sentiment by utilizing the language of benevolence and divine providence. In an 1858 visit, the board of supervisors agreed publicly that, "[the asylum] is indeed a noble institution" (*Daily Courier*). The asylum era in Syracuse was born by way of ceremonial acts that proclaimed stately and gallant visions that exalted the founders, the land, and the endeavor.

This noble and sentimental rhetoric however only came to bear on the asylum because of a decades-long stretch—with more to come—of claims by reformers, such as Dorothea Dix, that the lives of the "worthy" poor deserved improving. James Trent offers a chronology of how events following the Civil War, such as increased immigration and the Depression of 1873–79, strengthened the distinction between "worthy" and "unworthy" poor; "indoor" relief grew, which meant that, beginning in the 1820s, people, instead of receiving alms from the government, were increasingly placed in orphanages, residential schools (for the blind and deaf and also for the able-bodied), jails, and asylums. Culminating in Frederick Backus's 1851 memorial to the New York legislature to care for its "idiot" population, civil and rhetorical power had been rallying the state to build institutions for the "worthy" poor since since the 1830s, when the first laws were passed to more strictly legislate activity in poorhouses. The ceremony in Syracuse was just one of many examples of nobility and benevolence being called into play during this transition from the poorhouse to the asylum. Nobility and sanctimony would continue to typify much of the rhetoric of the first ten to fifteen years after the school's opening, although the noble rhetoric was complicated by other realities and other tropes, each of which formed an aspect of the arguments surrounding institutionalization.

The School

While contemporary notions of an asylum generally reverberate more with confinement tactics than with educational practices, the New York State Asylum for Idiots was in fact a school. Most of its rhetoric after the opening ceremony was educational. Nonetheless, asylums are rarely conceived of within an educational framework; this is a problem of historiography and memory. However, it is imperative to understand the early period at the New York State Asylum (approximately the first thirty years) as comprising a school because the original and relatively progressive educational practices of this asylum-school have in later years been overshadowed by warranted claims of civil and human rights violations. Asylums or "asylum-schools" as alternative educational settings are a part of a beleaguered past which we have failed to fully historicize because of the necessity of first exposing injustice. The asylum-school's opening in 1854 inaugurated what is often thought of as the first public school that offered what we know today as "special education." It exists simultaneously as a monument to a glorious past and a reminder of a reprehensible past.

While it is necessary to remember it as a school, it is a fraught endeavor to historicize the asylum that way. That is to say, it is misguided to call the institution a school past the time period I emphasize. Initially called the New York State Asylum for Idiots (1855), the institution changed its name to Syracuse State Institution for Feeble Minded Children (1891), then to the Syracuse State School for Mental Defectives (1920), after which it was known only as the Syracuse State School. It is ironic that by the 1920s, when the population of pupils rose to more than a thousand, educational practices almost entirely vanished and were replaced by custodialism, so that the institution functioned less like a school than it ever had, even though it was only then that it was officially labeled as such.

In its beginning, however, the asylum was aligned with the common school movement. For Wilbur more than anyone, in his tenure as superintendent during the first thirty years of the asylum from 1853 to 1883, it was a school; in his eyes his work was philosophically connected to the French Enlightenment, the struggle for individual rights, and the movement toward universal education. In this section, I will briefly contextualize the asylum-school in its beginnings first as an institution of learning with a trajectory similar to yet also divergent from the common school movement, and second, as an institution of learning that, toward the end of Superintendent Wilbur's life in 1883, began to replace its educational ideals with those of custodialism and industrial labor.

Early on, the educational rhetoric was robust: in the fourth *Annual Report*, Wilbur appealed to the legislature: "To be uneducated" he writes, "is to be in a degraded and painful condition" (4th *Annual Report*, 199). In contradiction to what was previously thought of as an irresolvable conundrum (an "educated idiot"), Wilbur professes that the "idiot" can learn. This claim alone was responsible for the asylum's first thirty years of educational practices. The mid-century phenomenon known as "idiot education" had crossed the Atlantic and arrived in Massachusetts and New York, and Syracuse would be its testing ground. The claim that "idiots" could learn aligned itself with Enlightenment thought: the individual was capable of vast improvement and all classes of people, including "idiots" (according to some), were deserving of a right to education as a means to improve morally and intellectually. In the *Report* of 1852, the trustees looked to the noble "idiot institutions" of France, Switzerland, Germany, and Britain that had been "crowned with abundant success" (33, 70). Horace Mann, known as the educator who played a central role in organizing the common school movement in Massachusetts, visited Europe to tour schools in 1848 with Samuel Gridley Howe,[6] comrade to Wilbur and founder of the famous Perkins Institute for the Blind, where Helen Keller was educated. Howe was also an abolitionist, fighter for the Greek Revolution, and advocate for women's rights. He and Wilbur traveled in the same professional circles. Horace Mann visited and attested to the success of the Syracuse experiment. Howe's testimony to the Massachusetts legislature in 1852 demonstrated an attempt to link "idiot education" with common schools. He testified that schools for "idiots" were "a link in the chain of common schools—the last indeed, but still one necessary in order to make the chain embrace all the children in the state" (Howe, 1852).

As this quote by Howe suggests, the asylum-school movement followed a trajectory that aligned it with the common school movement. Both the common school movement and the education of "idiots" followed in the theoretical footsteps of the French Enlightenment; both had similar philosophical roots devoted to overall improvement of the moral, physical, intellectual, and spiritual aspects of the child. Superintendent Wilbur brought attention to the implicit connection when he wrote, "It must be obvious to you, gentlemen [the board of trustees and the New York State Legislature], that many of the principles adopted in any judicious course of instruction for ordinary children will be equally applicable to our pupils" (1st *Annual Report*, 58). Though the asylum did not use the word *school* officially in its name until around 1920, Wilbur and other prominent figures such as Horace Mann and Samuel J. May[7] conferred educational status onto the asylum in a way that transformed how we conceive of asylums.

The common school movement led by Mann closely paralleled many educational reform movements for blind, deaf, and "idiotic" people. Mann was an avid supporter of "idiot education" and had studied the theories of Edouard Seguin, the philosophical father of the asylum-school (Winzer, 112). "Idiot education" was an extension of the common school in that it offered education to people not yet protected by laws of universal education, which wouldn't come into being until the 1970s.[8] In New York State, a compulsory education act for "ordinary" (synonymous with today's "normal") children was passed in 1874. The first Syracuse high school opened in 1876, though high school–level classes had begun there in 1854. The first Syracuse Board of Education met in 1848 (Roseboom, 132). It was said that the school system of Syracuse was free and open to all; yet simultaneously, analogous institutions for the blind, deaf, and "idiotic" were maintained at least partially because not all students were allowed to or able to attend the regular school.

The asylum followed in a tradition of schooling that had begun with those who were deaf. One of the first schools for blind, deaf, or "idiotic" people (those considered not "ordinary") was The Virginia School for the Deaf, which had opened in the 1780s but closed after a few years. In 1817, The American Asylum for Deaf-mutes at Hartford, now known as the American School for the Deaf, was founded by Thomas Hopkins Gallaudet and Laurent Clerc; today, it is the oldest permanent school (primary and secondary education) for deaf people in the United States. In 1818, the New York Institution for Deaf and Dumb opened, with a capacity for 550 pupils, in New York City. In 1832, Samuel Gridley Howe opened the Massachusetts Asylum for the Blind (now known as the Perkins School for the Blind), and in the same year another school for the blind was opened in New York City by Dr. John Russ, who had been in Greece with Howe and who gathered boys he had discovered at New York City almshouses and brought them under his supervision at the school (Winzer, 108). In *The History of Special Education*, Margaret Winzer goes on to list a tradition of "institutions for mentally retarded persons" as follows: In 1848, Hervey Wilbur opened a private school in his home in Barre, Massachusetts. After at least two years of working to identify and "solve the problem of idiocy," Howe established an experimental school for "idiotic" children in 1848 as a wing within the Massachusetts Asylum for the Blind, though it would last for only three years. It is said that Wilbur's private school in Barre predated Howe's school in Boston by a few months (Winzer, 114). By 1888, there were twelve institutions for "idiots" in the United States (Winzer, 103–15).

A compulsory public education act wouldn't pass again until 1909; it would require "refresher courses," provided by teachers who had undergone special training, for pupils who had been determined by Henry Goddard's version of the IQ test to be feeble-minded (around this period, the test was newly used as the official "intelligence" indicator) (Fletcher-Janzen, 407). By 1909, special education in common schools was the result. The next important law—The Education for All Handicapped Children Act (EHA), now known as the Individuals with Disabilities Education Act (IDEA)—would not be passed until 1974, almost one hundred years after the initial compulsory education laws for "ordinary" children were enacted. While there was a parallel trajectory between public schooling for able-bodied children and "idiot education" for disabled children, the educational realities that existed between the 1850s and 1880s directed them toward divergent ends. It was toward the end of Wilbur's tenure at Syracuse during the early 1880s that custodial and industrial goals achieved precedence over other, more specifically educational purposes.

Despite the philosophical and social links between common schools and asylum-schools, the asylum-schools' unique connection to medical rehabilitation complicated fundamental notions of schooling. The asylum was a medicalized space where biological pathology determined curriculum and treatment. In "A Pupil and a Patient," Brad Byrom uses the term *hospital-school* to describe "institutions that combined varying degrees of education (moral, vocational, and academic), socialization, and medical practice" (145). Mitchell and Snyder's *Cultural Locations of Disability* refers to the medico-pedagogic, which describes the confluence of institutional medical intervention with training and teaching techniques (95). But it is Henri Stiker, in *A History of Disability*, who most clearly delimits technologies of rehabilitation; his arguments help us understand how rehabilitation and medical practices appropriated and usurped the original educational intentions of the asylum-school. For Stiker, rehabilitation is a problem of production (170). That is, rehabilitation (re)produces preset norms. It produces a body and mind as identical as possible to those considered "ordinary" (the "normal" of today). Rehabilitation is a function of industrialization, in that the individual who requires rehabilitation needs to be made more productive. At the asylum-school, education and rehabilitation could be said to have moved in opposite directions: education, for Wilbur, enlightened the body, mind, and soul, while rehabilitation constituted a retrofitting (rehabilitation, from L. *habilis*, easily managed fit) of a person into some measurable norm.

The practices of rehabilitation and education do indeed overlap in the asylum-school. In the nineteenth century, the model called Moral Treatment epitomized the combination of these practices. Briefly, Moral Treatment has a lineage connected to multiple European intellectuals: William Tuke, the Quaker philanthropist and founder of the York Retreat for Idiots and the Insane in England (1796); Philippe Pinel, a French physician, disciple of Condillac, and often thought to be a founder of modern psychiatry; Jean-Marc Gaspard Itard, chief physician of the National Institution for Deaf-Mutes in Paris at the beginning of the nineteenth century and teacher of the famous case of the Wild Boy of Aveyron. The iconic story of the Wild Boy is important because it symbolizes the movement toward language teaching. Pinel thought the Wild Boy, a speechless youth found in a forest in France, to be an "incurable idiot." Itard, however, thought otherwise; thus, he commenced to teach the boy, in what is often thought to have been the beginning of modern special education.

Edouard Seguin, the French physician who came to the United States in 1848, is recognized as the first person to systematize education for "idiots"; Wilbur proclaimed his indebtedness to Seguin in the first *Annual Report* (57). Seguin, who also will be discussed in detail in chapter 3, shares ideologies with Pestalozzi and Montessori. Montessori's educational philosophy evolved out of work with "exceptional" children.

At first, the New York State Asylum for Idiots did in fact function much as a school, and when considered as such, it fits alongside other nineteenth-century residential schools whose rhetoric and pedagogy scholars are examining today in order to learn more about marginalized groups. As in Amanda J. Cobb's work on literacy and Native American education in the nineteenth century, study of the asylum-school points to ways in which "hidden curriculum" (Cobb's term) functions in education to acculturate. And as in David Gold's study of a black liberal arts college, a public women's college, and an independent teacher training school, the asylum-school may be studied as a location where we can look for innovative practices having to do with civic participation in nontraditional sites.

Examination of the rationale behind the asylum-school illuminates instances of the ways rehabilitation, medical, and custodial practices merged with, and overtook, educational practices. The asylum-school is a nontraditional educational setting that redefines what we mean when we speak of schooling. Learning was the core feature of the curriculum in the early years, and this is important because public arguments made for the creation and maintenance of asylums did not foresee the custodialization and warehousing that was to come in the late nineteenth and early twentieth century. The rhetoric of the asylum-school's founding was vigorously educational: in order to justify the institution, it had to be proven that the "idiot" could learn and that the curriculum and its achievements paralleled the common school and the residential school of the nineteenth century.

The Prison

While the asylum was in many senses a school, it was primarily an asylum which in the popular view today bears a carceral connotation. The sentimental, noble, and educational rhetoric of the school was contradicted by multiple other available versions of the asylum, which dispensed discipline in ways similar to prisons and residential boarding schools. Before explaining how pupils were selected for the asylum, and some of the particulars of its geography and space, here I briefly discuss some of the essential components of the asylum that are reminiscent of prison and boarding school geographies.

Even without a wall surrounding the institution's acreage, a clear split would have been felt between the asylum and the community. Data in almost every annual report indicate that "runaways" and pupils who left the grounds without permission were a persistent problem. In light of the asylum's identity as an inviolable, entirely separate, and mechanized place, what were the discursive and material effects of such arrangements? Interestingly, these ritualized mechanisms were not unique to the New York State Asylum; in fact, many other residential schools for people both with and without disabilities (schools for the deaf, Indian schools, women's colleges, normal schools, boarding schools) during this time period would have operated in ways similar to residential schools, which I have laid out in chapter 3. The "idiot asylum" was epitomized by: one, pupils who were viewed as seriously deficient in physical and mental abilities, and two, pupils who often lacked the power to communicate (because of deafness, processing ability, or speech issues).

Under the control of a central management system, embodied in a panopticon-like structure, the pupil at the asylum-school operated within mechanisms of ritualized discipline reminiscent of Victorian schooling and the utilitarianism of Jeremy Bentham's prison model. A clearly delineated hierarchy was maintained, with the superintendent-physician (Dr. Wilbur) at the top, followed by nurses, teachers, matrons, groundskeepers, servants, and pupils. In the asylum, humanity was quantified and recorded meticulously in logbooks, evaluation reports, payroll lists, patient admission files, laundry lists, possession indicators, progress reports, attitude meters, visitation registries, clothing inventories, distribution registries, gift registries, and toileting schedules. Mealtimes were ritualized and formalized. The body was continually evaluated and gazed upon (as the section on *the described* will demonstrate). Movement was limited to certain spaces; for example, a "high picket fence" was built around the institution in 1857 in order to contain the "runaways" that were listed in the previous year's annual report. Visits home were only allowed when the pupil's family had enough time and the money to pay for transportation and secure the pupil's position upon his or her return (*Thornton Letters*).

As Michel Foucault might ask: What is the meaning of the ritual divisions upon which the asylum was organized? By briefly exploring the work of Foucault and social science theorist Erving Goffman, I wish to develop an initial picture of the asylum model as embodying a ritualized and historically contextualized style of training. The asylum model is grounded in the idea that by physically segregating a class or multiple classes of people, society *and* the individual might improve. This move to improve is embedded in ritualized acts of discipline and punishment, and here asylum practices merge with carceral practices. Foucault's notions of *biopower* and Goffman's notion of *total institutions* help to elucidate the asylum model as prison-like; furthermore, their theories counter the arguments for benevolent reform, which utilized the sentimental and epideictic rhetoric that composed so much of the public discourse about institutionalization in the nineteenth century. However, I am less interested at this point in offering arguments against institutionalization, though that is important; rather, I wish to call attention to the broad historical principles of asylums and the localized realities of this asylum in particular.

The breadth of Foucault's work relating to institutions can only be acknowledged in passing here; most importantly, he posits a deep historical lineage for the practice of separating people out of communities and relocating them in isolation. And even though Foucault's genealogy centers around discursive formations, he is always also signifying material circumstances. In *Madness and Civilization* (1961), Foucault tells us that assembling people based on similar characteristics was not a phenomenon new to the nineteenth century. Army forts, for example, have been a part of European culture for at least three thousand years, and monasteries for close to two thousand. Foucault takes us back to medieval times in Europe and differentiates between the exclusion of lepers who were expelled from their communities and the plague victims who were segregated in almshouses. He discusses the Ship of Fools as a reiterative historical ideology that included the practice of putting people identified as unwanted or undesirable out to sea.

For Foucault, the unwanted typically meant the madman. But Foucault's work on madness is relevant to "idiocy" because prior to the nineteenth century, "insanity" and "idiocy" were often conflated. Both categories were constructed around a person's assumed lack of reason. And for the first time, in the classical period, he asserts, society tried to cure madness. The Great Confinement began, according to Foucault, with the Hôpital Général in Paris in 1656; confinement came when the desire for cure arose. Confinement, it was argued, could then bring about improvement, even cure, more easily because people could be disciplined or reformed methodically and without the distraction of the temptations of the world. In *The Unfit: The History of a Bad Idea,* Elof Carlson goes even farther back than Foucault, to the Amalekites in the Old Testament who are thought to have separated out and condemned people to death because of their so-called depravity and lack of fitness for reproduction.

Foucault's work more generally was concerned with how "abnormal" behavior (madness, masturbation, homosexuality) came under state control through the diffuse use of power. Starting in the nineteenth century, Foucault linked a new vision of the city with new attitudes toward poverty, work (idleness), and the move toward differentiation between "normals" and "deviants." Madness has always been an archetype, but with the development of psychiatry and sociology in the nineteenth century, madness became an unacceptable limit of reality; though Foucault does not mention it by name, "idiocy" did in fact follow suit. More than *Madness and Civilization, Discipline and Punish* exposes how confinement of "abnormals" enacted "biopower." The body within prison and asylum systems has no analytic certainty, but rather is constituted by discursive formations. According to Shelley Tremain, who is known for her critical readings of Foucault through the lens of disability studies, *biopower* is "the endeavor to rationalize the problems that the phenomena characteristic of a group of living human beings, when constituted as a population, pose to governmental practice. . . . [B]io-power is then the strategic movement of relatively recent forms of power/knowledge towards an increasingly comprehensive management of these problems" ("On the Government of Disability," 185). Bodies are disciplined through the art of distributions wherein rote mechanisms control arrangements of time and space and the positions of bodies. There is uninterrupted, constant coercion; the docile body is used and improved.

Goffman depicts a related scene in *Asylums: Essays on the Social Situation of Mental Patients and Other Inmates* (1961). The self of the inmate is degraded, mortified, and humiliated as he or she is admitted and adapts (14). For Goffman, a total institution is "a place of residence and work where a large number of like-situated individuals, cut off from the wider society for an appreciable period of time, together lead an enclosed, formally administered round of life" (xiii). Bodies are confined; power is asserted over the inmate. Furthermore, (1) every function of life is conducted in the same place under one single, stable authority; (2) all daily activities are performed in the company of others, and all people, in some sense, are treated alike; (3) all activities take place on a tight timetable and there are formal rules governing behavior and action; (4) the institution is governed by one single plan designed to fulfill its goal. Mortification of the self involves the destruction of the patient's "identity kit," which includes personal items such as clothes and hygiene supplies (20).

As the patient adjusts to the discipline of the total institution, an "underlife of the institution" develops (see chapter 4 on the underlife of the archive); inmates perform unauthorized actions. Some flee or resist. The prison-like apparatus hides behind the public face of the institution and its noble and sentimental rhetoric. It is the alternatives to the benevolent rhetoric that I examine in the rest of this chapter: the way pupils are viewed and the way they are constructed via biopower. Some of the benevolent rhetoric loses its distinction as the day to day practices of the asylum take hold and the noble sentiments fade. That is, the materiality of the asylum as it is often contrasts with the idea of the noble asylum as it is thought to be. The asylum is pastoral; the pupil is described, counted, nameless, visited, and displayed.

The Described and the Counted

While discussion of the noble asylum, the asylum as a school, and the asylum as carceral centralize around the institution, in the rest of this chapter I examine the how "idiocy" was further constructed rhetorically through complex and reiterative arguments made by reformers and educators. These arguments became commonplaces; the tropes of *the described and the counted* were in fact so fundamental to the construction and maintenance of the asylum that without them there was no "idiot asylum"—Goffman's notion of the *total institution* and Foucault's *art of distributions* and notion of *biopower* are categorically part of these tropes. Reformers and educators described and counted pupils so pervasively that we can easily acquaint ourselves with the pupils of the asylum-school both through secondhand, professionalized bodily and behavioral description and through statistical measurement. The "idiot" is edified for us through description and enumeration so comprehensively that individuals merge into a unified group from which generalizations can succinctly be wrought. I analyze the traditional techniques of reporting that were recorded by the institution and the government (in annual reports, government documents, and newspaper articles) and examine the statistical, enumerative, and descriptive data for its own rhetorical bent.

Who attended the asylum-school? How were the pupils identified and selected, and how did they qualify for admittance? How did definition lead to description and enumeration, which then generated more description and more enumeration . . . ad infinitum? Exploring these questions points to how measurement and differentiation were deployed to rhetorically construct the pupils. An "idiot" was someone who, by Wilbur's definition, appeared or behaved outside of "ordinary" parameters. The line of reasoning he fashioned goes as follows: "idiocy" is x (definition), this person is x (verified by description), this person is not y, therefore this person is an "idiot" (and so are all these other people)—which teaches us that "idiocy" is largely the product of rhetoric. After the "idiot" was initially reified through definition, then by description, enumeration ensued, followed by more description. Through this reiterative reasoning, Wilbur and the trustees of the asylum constructed a reality for what constituted the "idiot."

Superintendent Wilbur's widely circulated definitions of "idiocy" are important indices for assessing intellect and physiologic function. His theories would have been widely accepted among physicians, as Wilbur was highly respected in the growing subfield of medicine that studied and treated "idiocy." For Wilbur, "idiocy" was "the want of a natural or harmonious development of the mental, active and moral powers of a human being, and usually dependent upon some defect or infirmity of his nervous organization" (1st *Annual Report*, 49). Wilbur goes on to explain:

> In the case of ordinary children, all the natural channels of communication between the mind and the external world are open. In addition, the mind sits alive and awake to receive and appropriate to itself the facts and phenomena communicated through those senses. Sensation is a law of their being; perception is the next natural step from sensation; and memory, comparison and judgment as naturally follow. Educated by these simple intellectual operations, their minds turn inwardly, and with the exercise of consciousness, become capable of comprehending the laws of mind. Their wills undergo a simultaneous development, through the reciprocating influences of intelligence and will. In the case of our pupils, as we have seen, these natural avenues between the mind and the world of relation are more or less obstructed: and not only so, but the mind itself, inert and feeble, sleeps while the dull sensations are calling faintly for entrance. Their sensations are imperfect; they awaken no perceptions, or if any, but indistinct and limited, and

> consequently faint and feeble will be, if any, the mental operations that follow. (1st *Annual Report*, 57)

Both of Wilbur's definitions point to "idiocy" as a physiological, sensorial, and nervous system–affected state—a state that Wilbur believed could be modified through education and training. "Idiocy" of this physiological type, he thought, could be removed or "cured" through restoration of the nervous system; control over the nervous system would bring about a more conscious and reflective mind. Chapter 3 will discuss in detail the physiological education that Wilbur adopted, via Edouard Seguin, to train his pupils, as a means to treat their "idiocy." Since the Binet metric intelligence scale (IQ test) was not used until 1905, in Wilbur's time physiologic function was regarded as an indicator of intelligence (Fletcher-Janzen, 407).[9]

Essentially, by arguing that "idiots" were "wanting" in "the powers of a human being," Wilbur was in fact arguing that although they did have those powers at some level, they had not developed them sufficiently to function. Wilbur writes,

> [I]t should be remembered that they have a human origin; that however they may differ in physical, mental or moral organization they are yet human beings; that their degradation in the scale of humanity, however it may modify, constitutes no absolute release or outlawry from the duties or rights which belong to them as human beings, and finally, that they have a human soul, a human destiny. (1st *Annual Report*, 56)

Rhetorically, "idiocy" was constructed through Wilbur's paradoxical vision: "idiots" were miserably degraded but teachable, human but immoral. With these parameters in place, potential candidates for classification in the category of "idiocy" generally, and for the asylum-school specifically, could be identified.

The process of admitting pupils was idiosyncratic to say the least: in order to be admitted as a pupil, a child first would have to be identified as an "idiot" by a physician from the town where the child lived. This determination to be based on Wilbur's parameters, accompanied by a description of physical traits and physiological function. After the physician had verified the child's eligibility for candidacy, then a family member or friend would seek application to the school on the child's behalf. The First Annual Report of 1852 goes on to explain how pupils were found: each trustee of the board, of which there were eight, excluding Governor Washington Hunt, was assigned a district. In each district, the trustee was asked to dispatch circulars to gentlemen (overseers of poorhouses, physicians, other prominent men) of the fifty-six counties seeking "idiot" children under twelve years of age. From these enumerations and from other applications submitted by the families, physicians, and "friends" of "idiots," a list was compiled (1st *Annual Report,* 9). Selection criteria are articulated in a later report of 1863: "Children between the ages of seven and fourteen, who are idiotic or so deficient in intelligence as to be incapable of being educated at any ordinary school, and who are not epileptic, insane or greatly deformed, may be admitted by the Superintendent with the advice and consent of the Executive Committee. Applications in behalf of others shall be referred to the action of the Board of Trustees" (12th *Annual Report,* 73).

In the early years of the school, Superintendent Wilbur believed that no one was unteachable; he admitted children across the spectrum of economic status and across the spectrum of the designation of "idiocy." In the asylum-school's first annual report of 1852, the trustees explain that while any "idiot" was permitted entry into the asylum, for those admitted, there were "no restrictions as to the degree of "idiocy" (12). That the scope of who was admitted was vast tells us that the parameters Wilbur envisioned for "idiocy" were far-reaching and flexible in how they were understood.

Once admitted to the school, the pupil was assessed by Wilbur in terms of physiological function through observation and description (related to the rhetorical strategies of *effictio* and *ethopoeia*). The assessment included evaluation of how well or "ordinarily" a child could speak, read, listen, follow commands, respond, walk, sit upright, eat, dress, willingly move the head and limbs, and control the eyes (Pupil Evaluation Reports). Wilbur's extensive physical and behavioral descriptions of pupils in the early annual reports demonstrate not only the admission criteria for the school but also bring us closer to some sort of limited knowledge of the pupils themselves. In the 1852 report, Wilbur notes that out of twenty-five pupils that were admitted in 1851, it was reported that twelve could not speak at all. Of the pupils who were without speech, six had "no idea of language" and also could not comprehend speech. The method Wilbur used to determine when a child failed to comprehend speech is unknown. Of those who could speak, three spoke with difficulty, and two did not speak at all until they were nine years old and then with just a few words. It is reported that seven walked imperfectly, three had partial paralysis, eleven had experienced convulsions, eight had excessive flow of saliva, seven were "inattentive to the calls of nature," five were irritable, some were unable to dress themselves, and only four, according to Wilbur, "could feed themselves with propriety. . . . None of them could read or write, or count, or distinguish colors by name" (1st *Annual Report,* 44–45). The pupils showed "imperfect physical organization," with a few variations in appearance from a regular head or face. Some had a wandering gaze while others had vacant eyes. Some were restless, others inert (51).

That the asylum relocated to a building in Syracuse in 1852 that had an entranceway with steps—I have found no mention of a ramp or reference to wheelchairs—confirms that the asylum-school's admittance criteria probably leaned toward more physically abled pupils. The 1852 report goes on to say that the children admitted were below average in intelligence in relation to other "idiots" in the state; it was this "deficiency" that brought these specific pupils to "avail themselves of the State charity" (1st *Annual Report,* 47). Wilbur adds, "In general terms our pupils may be described as affectionate, mild and obedient and easily amused or rendered happy (ibid., 53)." This portrayal of willing, demure applicants served to distinguish "idiots" from the insane, who otherwise were portrayed as wild and untamed. The differentiation between the "idiotic" and the insane was important in this context because each class could receive their own unique form of moral treatment and (re)education. Physical and physiological description operated as part of a rhetoric of admittance that gave pupils access to education and rehabilitation at the asylum-school.

Besides description, "idiocy" was consolidated by enumeration. People who were described as having "unordinary" physical and physiological features and functions could thus be counted as "idiots" and, although differing greatly from one another, could then be grouped together as a distinct class of people. Multiple forms of enumeration came along once definitions of "idiocy" were concretized and circulated. Wilbur assured the legislature that the assignment of "these unfortunates" into a class by themselves would not cost society much but rather would benefit everyone (17th *Annual Report,* 13).

In 1850, four years prior to the school's opening in Syracuse, the U.S. census for the first time had counted "idiots." The 1850 census, also for the first time, counted family members other than heads of households. Categories in the 1850 census included name, address, age, sex, color (black, white, or mulatto), deaf, dumb, blind, insane, or "idiotic"; the census inquired whether respondents had married within the previous year, whether they had attended school within the year, whether those over twenty could read or write, whether they were paupers or convicts. Yet in the First Annual Report it is written that "[t]he census returns included idiots and lunatics in the same class" (9). This does not appear to have been the case, however, as the enclosed census document clearly shows deaf and dumb, blind, insane, and idiotic all enumerated as separate categories. Invariably, disagreements existed over what constituted each category, which resulted in disagreements over statistical measurement.

Regardless, in the state of New York, the census of 1850 reported 1,665 "idiots" out of a total population of 3,097,304 (a negligible percentage). The further breakdown of "idiocy" went as follows: 961 white males, 683 white females, 9 free colored males, 12 free colored females. Out of that total, 1,328 were reported to have been born in the state, 164 born out of state, though in the United States, and 161 born in foreign countries. Out of this total, 49,069 were free blacks. Enslaved African Americans were not among the counted in any category since slavery had ended in New York in 1827. While the population of people born in other countries was 655,929 (21 percent of the total population), only 10 percent of those counted as "idiots" were foreign born (161/1665). While it is clear that the 1850 census did in fact distinguish between "idiots" and "lunatics," it is less clear how those determinations were made. At the asylum-school, a pupil was typically dismissed if insanity was considered a factor. Nonetheless, the board of trustees did not find the census data sufficient, both because the trustees (perhaps wrongly) claimed that "idiocy" and lunacy were combined and because they claimed the numbers were underestimations. The trustees wrote that it would, therefore,

> be necessary to obtain accurate information on these points, before definite action can be had. And we would respectfully submit to the Legislature the propriety of requiring the assessors of the towns and wards and cities, to ascertain the number, age, sex and condition in respect to health, of all idiots within their assessment districts; and of requiring the superintendents of alms houses, county and town poor houses to make similar returns of the idiots under their charge. (1st *Annual Report*, 4)

The enumeration of "idiots" by the census was important to the asylum because it gave the asylum's advocates ammunition for their argument that the target population not only existed but was in need of a school. Also, if numbers increased, it could be argued that the previous numbers had been erroneously low and that the need for the institution was increasing. Wilbur believed the estimate found in the 1850 census accounted for only half of the number of "idiots" in the state. The Annual Report of 1854 suggests that measures be taken to count the proper number, but also that a law for that purpose had been rightfully passed (12). Often, lists compiled by the state were sent to the asylum-school and if only a few names were recognized by Wilbur and other staff members the count was determined to be incorrect. In this way, the asylum-school acted as a state-sponsored channel through which not only the definition of "idiocy" would pass but enumeration of "idiots" too.

Consistent enumeration and description of pupils within the asylum were key parts of every annual report to the legislature both to sustain bids for funding and to show that as the numbers increased, the facilities required enlargement. In 1851, when the asylum was still located in Albany, twenty-five pupils lived there. The original act passed by the legislature to establish the asylum-school in 1848 limited the number of state pupils to twenty; however, the Annual Report of 1852 lists a pupil population of twenty-three (9), and in 1852, the number of pupils had grown to forty-six. The Fourth Annual Report of 1854 lists fifty pupils, and in 1856, "There are now between eighty and ninety pupils connected with the Asylum" (5th *Annual Report*, 62). Then the numbers increased as follows: ninety in 1857; 140 in 1863; 143 in 1867; 150 in 1871. The size of the population at the asylum would become increasingly important as the asylum grew, as Wilbur used the pupil population in two ways: he cited the steadily increasing numbers, first, in requesting increased funding to enlarge the buildings and hire more employees, and second, to show that the services provided by the asylum-school were increasingly in demand.

Besides emphasizing the precise number of pupils present, the Annual Report "rated" the pupils in terms of their masculinity. Masculinity typically served as a measure of work productivity. A man was someone who could work independently and efficiently. Case No. 11, for example, first gives the physical description of the pupil, judges his work productivity, then rates his masculinity: "J. O. a boy of 13 years old; very tall of his age; good looking: Works very good on the farm. He would be rated by the steward of the asylum as two-thirds a man" (15th *Annual Report*, 45). Boys, who typically constituted two-thirds of the population of the school, were repeatedly evaluated based on manliness: Wilbur writes that in the pupils, "we see increased manifestation of observation, judgment, manliness, self control, and sense of propriety" (16th *Annual Report*; 17th *Annual Report*, 26). By singling out manliness when referring to the general population of pupils (which was both male and female), goals to achieve masculinity were foregrounded. Mention was often made of jobs that boys obtained after leaving the school as well as their service in the military. It is not determined whether girls' vocational experiences outside the asylum were not named because during this period they did not work off the asylum grounds or simply because these experiences were not recorded during this time period.

In addition to evaluation of masculinity by the institution, boys also evaluated their own manliness. In the 1866 annual report, Case No. 27, E. S., assures in a letter that when he becomes a man he will visit the asylum. After eight months at the school, he had returned home and did not wish to go back. It was an honor to be connected with the asylum-school, but one he did not wish to experience again in person until he reached manhood.

Manhood accorded him license to come and go as he pleased, rather than stay on possibly against his will. These gendered rhetorics point to the fact that gender expectations and norms were indeed important in the asylum. Females and males were measured and described in normative gendered ways in addition to the ones mentioned above where boys were measured based on independence, strength, and hard physical labor (such as farmwork and construction) and girls were measured based on interdependence, domestic labor, and modestness.

More measurements were ordered in the 1863 act passed by the legislature to reorganize the asylum. In his testimony regarding the proposed act, Wilbur declared there should be a bound book that recorded all the asylum's doings. The act also increased the number of bylaws of the institution, one of which formalized requests for admissions (106–108). The 1863 reorganization act states that "[t]he superintendent shall, at the time of the admission of any pupil into the Asylum, enter in a book to be printed and kept for that purpose, a minute, with date, of the name and residence of the pupil, and of the person or persons upon whose application he is received; together with a copy of the application, statement, certificate and all other papers accompanying such "idiot;" the originals of which he shall file and carefully preserve" (12th *Annual Report*, 99). This signifies that perhaps case records, case descriptions, and admission reports had not been recorded nor maintained with such precision prior to the act.

We know the pupils proximally through enumeration and medical description of their bodies and behaviors. In the 1853 Report, Wilbur details twelve cases that he says are based on reports sent to the asylum by family physicians or on the written testimony of parents or friends. Much more numerical and descriptive information is available, such as how many pupils paid how much and how many pupils were fully funded by the state, or the number of teachers, or the amount spent annually on farm production. These descriptions of bodies and behaviors and the obsessive enumeration of almost every aspect of the "idiot" and the "idiot asylum" demonstrate that the acts of describing and enumerating form the commonplace arguments that I characterize as "the described" and "the counted." The tropes rely upon inventive definitional and comparative lines of argument. An "idiot" was someone who was wanting in "natural or harmonious development of the mental, active and moral powers of a human being" (1st *Annual Report*, 49). An "idiot" was *not* someone who, in Wilbur's language, appeared or behaved within "ordinary" parameters. The line of reasoning—that "idiocy" is x (definition), this person is x (verified by description), this person is not y, therefore this person is an "idiot" (and so are all these other people)—teaches us that "idiocy" was largely the product of symbolic, definitional, and comparative reasoning. The tropes I call *the described and the counted* are rhetorical in the sense that they were used to make the argument that "idiocy" was real and in need of modification. Without these rhetorical moves to define, differentiate, and enumerate, there was no "idiot" and no "idiot asylum."

The Nameless Idiot

Like the tropes of *the described and the counted, the nameless idiot,* or the trope of anonymity, epitomizes another commonplace that coalesced to construct and maintain asylums. While *the described and the counted* worked around a definitional, descriptive, and comparative line of reasoning, the "idiot" as nameless and anonymous was set up as antithetical to the recognized professional, whose name was publicly well known and who held the title of Superintendent or Physician. What did it means to be (un)known? While efficiently described and counted in the ways I have indicated above, today the pupils and their families are largely unidentifiable by name in the historical record. The rhetoric of anonymity is epitomized within a complicated line of arguments. But this Nameless One is not a sacred or holy individual; rather, to be unknown is to be known in the terms set forth by the asylum system. To illuminate the rhetorical nature of anonymity, I return to Goffman's notion of total institutions. In Goffman's discussion of the "moral career" of the inmate, the self is not constituted by the self but rather by institutional arrangement and social control. For Goffman, the self merges against anything other than itself, yet also the self "resides in the cracks" of the walls of the institution (319–20). The asylum strips identity away from the inmate and supplants it with anonymity. Anonymity in the asylum-school offers a unique illustration of how the use of language by this particular institution submerges the self of the pupil or inmate.[10]

The question, *Who attended the asylum-school?* becomes even more complicated here. Much of the lives of the pupils exists in anonymous line items. The rhetoric of anonymity is discernable in the following "List of State Pupils in the Asylum":

> Dist. No. 1. N. M., W. McC., J. M., city of New-York.
> do. 2. H. H., A. P., Brooklyn, Kings co.
> do. 3. E. D., Ulster co., C. A., Columbia co., C. L., Albany co.
> do. 4. A. M., St. Lawrence co., H. G., Washington co., (C., Franklin co., selected, not arrived.)
> do. 5. S. F., Jefferson co., (G. W., from Oneida co., selected, not arrived.)
> do. 6. O. B., Madison co., J. C., Oswego co. (There are two pending applications from this district, one of which will be granted.)

do. 7. W. C., Ontario co., M. S., Seneca co.
do. 8. E. A. C., Cattarangus co. (1st *Annual Report,* 24).

This list is daunting in its coded language. Each pupil is listed by initials followed by the city or county from which they were "selected." Each pupil is numbered in the list. Following the list, the report notes:

> [Regard for the future interests of the pupils and for the feelings of their relatives has induced the substitution of the initial letters of their names instead of giving them at length. They will be furnished, however, to any member of the Legislature, on application to the Executive committee or to the Superintendent]. (1st *Annual Report,* 26)

This reveals that the trustees removed the names intentionally. It tells us that the legislature was understood to have been only one audience for the report, which seemingly had a larger public audience. The trustees felt they had to protect the identities of the pupils and their families, although the legislature was privy to the names if and when they desired them. People were often kept anonymous because it was considered correct practice even prior to the twentieth century HIPAA (Health Insurance Portability and Accountability Act) patient privacy laws. This attempt to maintain privacy through anonymity is repeated throughout the annual reports. Other examples of anonymity that protected privacy may be found in letters reprinted in the annual reports that were written and signed by family members inquiring about their relatives. In the 15th Annual Report of 1866, it is stated that a letter of an eighteen-year-old pupil writing to their mother could be reprinted because no name was on the letter (15th *Annual Report,* 45).

The rhetoric of at least partial anonymity is also apparent in the use of only first names in detailed case descriptions (which were similar to case histories). In *Patient Tales,* Carol Berkenkotter offers an extensive analysis of the ways that nineteenth-century case histories were narrative in form, and that is likewise true here. The asylum case descriptions are informal stories that use a first name to, so to speak, personalize the narrative and thereby make the case more real to the legislature. Description of Cases Nos. 8 and 9[11] gives an idea of what constituted a case description: it tells where the pupils were found and how their expenses were paid, and offers physical and physiological descriptions:

> Cases No. 8 and 9 "Natty and Willie—boys of 7 and 8 years old, taken from what is called the idiot-house, on Randall's Island, an island occupied by the alms-house department of the city of

> New-York, for the residence of the children supported at the city's expense. There were no applications from the first judicial district at the opening of the asylum, and I, in company with one of the board, of trustees, visited the island. These two were selected on account of their age. Both had been regarded as idiots from birth; both were partially paralyzed; both entirely dumb, though comprehending some simple commands, and the names of a few familiar objects. The resident physician of the establishment, who was absent when I made the selection, thought it an unfortunate one, as he feared the pupils in question would never do any credit to the new State charity. They made their appearance, however, on the 14th of December, 1851, in company with another child taken from a cellar in New-York city." (2nd *Annual Report*, 140–42)

Superintendent Wilbur explained, broadly, what elements case descriptions should include: "Besides this tabular statement of the condition of the pupils admitted, a description of each child is prepared, giving more details, illustrating their peculiarities" (3rd *Annual Report*, 75). The case descriptions generally included: age, appearance, stature, illnesses, language ability, energy level, state before and after admittance, and degree of usefulness. Case descriptions did not create subjectivity of the pupils but rather were designed to demonstrate for the legislature the benevolence at work in the school and its utility. Case descriptions tell how the school saved the pupils from the "wretched conditions" from which they came. No full names were needed for this purpose nor would it have been considered ethical practice to include the full names.

Anonymity also worked in asylum management to mechanize the system, so that it was not necessarily a pupil's individuality that mattered but rather the ability of management to generalize the subject's experience. In other words, anonymity was needed in order to describe and count "idiots." As one entered the system of excessive enumeration and description, one's name was abandoned. As Goffman has it, anonymity is part of a forced mortification of the self that destroys a person's "identity kit" (20). Even more overtly, anonymity appears in numerous logbooks that list people, literally, as line items (Log Books). The endless pages are arranged in columns of statistics listing countable categories—and no names—such as the numbers of incoming and outgoing inmates, escapes, paroles, and deaths. The logbooks are tightly bound in leather and have survived quite well. It is most noticeable that the only names that appear throughout these logbooks are the names of the employees who maintained the records. Likewise, the names of the teachers, groundskeepers, and farm employees have been included in the records available to me. Nevertheless, it is important to note that these logbooks are from the period of 1918–1938, so practices certainly must have changed since the early years of the asylum, and certainly record-keeping methods tightened after the 1863 administrative reorganization.

I am not the only person looking to make known what has been unknown. For example, there is a blog posting on rootsweb.ancestry.com in which a family member is asking for any records or sources regarding the Rochester Poorhouse, and seeking information on Willis Snyder or his family. This cannot be the Willie of Case No. 9 from the 1854 report, because the dates are wrong. The posting goes on to say that Snyder was born in 1881, orphaned in 1884, possibly sent to the asylum-school in 1889, then perhaps released to Monroe County Poorhouse in 1895 (freepages.genealogy.rootsweb.ancestry.com). Other remnants I have found outside the archives include a girl named Cora Tilyon, who was listed in the 1880 census of Masonville, in Delaware City, New York, and subsequently sent to the asylum-school. Her family is listed in the census as follows: John C., WM 43, Jane, WF 38, John W., 16, WF 13, Cora, WF 6, Albert, WM 4. From other county records: in 1889 a man named Elmer E. Fuller and a woman named Emma E. Fuller were transferred from Delaware County Poorhouse as paupers to the asylum in 1888; it is not known whether they were siblings or spouses. By the 1880s older inmates were accepted into the asylum; John Cuff went from Delaware County to the asylum in 1886 and then from Tompkins County Poorhouse in 1888 and 1889 (www.dcnyhistory.org/jouce/paupers.html). Even when full names are retrievable, information is scant.

The pupil as nameless and anonymous is another reiterated trope in the history of the asylum-school, and while there is a sense that the inmate may have been able to salvage or at least preserve some sense of him- or herself, we have yet to see it in the historical record. To be (un)known was to serve the larger purposes of the institution. An "idiot" was seemingly not to be remembered except in the terms of the institution, because effacement was part of what it meant to be construed as an "idiot," and within that effacement, the self cannot survive. This is the argument that lies within the trope of the *nameless idiot*. Anonymity further epitomizes the line of arguments thus: we protect the pupils by keeping them nameless; we identify the pupils in particularized and controlled ways that serve to fund and advance the institution; the pupils cannot be known for who they are but rather for what part of them will be rehabilitated; names should not be associated with "idiocy" even after it has been "cured" because "idiocy" is a shameful designation. This trope of the nameless reveals the nature of the historical record wherein an asylum pupil's home county is known but his or her gravestone is numbered and nameless.

The trope of anonymity was born but certainly did not end at the asylum-school. It was further established as a commonplace in Henry Goddard's 1912 eugenics tract called *The Kallikak Family*, where he situates a "nameless, feeble-minded girl" as his centerpiece. Goddard argues that this "nameless, feeble-minded girl" had illicit, extramarital relations with Martin Kallikak Senior. "Five generations of idiots" later, Deborah Kallikak appears as an inmate at the Vineyard Training School (an "idiot school") in New Jersey. Goddard goes on to argue that if this *nameless idiot* had been institutionalized in an asylum, she would never have given birth to so many feeble-minded defectives (104): "This defective family would not have existed" (ibid). In his heredity charts depicting the blood line of the Kallikaks, Goddard lists the names in the succeeding generations but not the name of the source of the feeble-mindedness herself—the nameless feeble-minded girl. Thus, she becomes an anonymous symbol of "idiocy." This trope can be found over and over in the construction of "idiocy" and is certainly still a commonplace today.

The Visited and the Displayed

Like anonymity, the tropes of visitation and display give rise to a host of significations: Who can visit whom? Who looks and who is the object of looking? How were these mechanisms part of the rhetoric that governed institutionalization? While the trope of the nameless gives and takes away one's identity, the tropes of the visited and the displayed regulate boundaries and spaces and create a sense of "looking" and "being looked at." The visited and the displayed work as circumstantial lines of reasoning that determine what is possible. The visitor—an advocate, a family member, an educator, a state employee, or a supporter—comes and goes, and gazes; the visited remains and is displayed and looked at. Indeed, visitation and display aided in the rhetorical construction of the "idiot" as a verifiable reality.

The reform work of Dorothea Dix (1802–1887), an advocate for the insane and "idiotic," provides an example that is paramount to understanding the complexities of the rhetoric employed in the mid-nineteenth century to build public support for asylums by way of visitation. By 1847, Dix had visited eighteen state penitentiaries, three hundred jails and houses of correction, and more than five hundred almshouses (Tiffany, 132). Her *Memorial to the Honorable Legislature of the State of New York* (Albany, Jan. 12, 1844) was delivered by a prominent male political figure, since women were not encouraged to speak in public venues (see Buchanan). In the statement, Dix begins by announcing that she speaks, in particular, for "this unfortunate class" of "idiots" and insane women who cannot care for themselves; they need protection from the sins of the poorhouse, she argues. For Dix, it is in the name of justice that she—and her legislative audience—is urged to take action to protect them. Following her affirmations of duty and pleas for justice, Dix gives extensive descriptions (once again, the trope of *the described*) of forty-three county poorhouses in the state of New York and also describes the insufficient conditions at a few newly constructed asylums. Relating her visit to the Onondaga County Poorhouse in Syracuse, she writes,

> I regret to refer to this establishment, since I cannot describe it advantageously in any respect. It compares very ill with most county-houses in general appearance, and arrangement. All the apartments needed complete cleansing by white-washing, scrubbing, and the renewing of much of the bed-clothing. The aspect of the whole place was that of discomfort; the sick needed more efficient care; the aged and blind more attention; the children some person to have them in sole charge; and the insane needed everything. I found the women in cells in wretched conditions. (*Memorial*, 31–32).

Dix's rhetoric revolved around a succinct set of actions that were loci for the tropes of the visited and displayed: visits and written observations (testimony and witnessing) followed by the delivery of those observations to state legislatures. Dix successfully used visitations and eyewitness accounts to argue for the "rescue" of inmates, including "idiots," from poorhouses. Her rhetoric also aided in creating "idiots" as a separate class of people from the insane. And though her use of visitations differed from Superintendent Wilbur's use, Dix's testimony, obtained through her visitations to city and county poorhouses and jails and prisons across the country, helped to redirect public support from poorhouses to asylums. Dix was responsible for much institutional building of the period. Her work demonstrates how civil power rallied the state toward institution building.

As abuses in the poorhouse were exposed via visitations,[12] funding for asylums increased. It would take continual and persistent visits throughout the nineteenth century to more fully discredit the poorhouse and, by exposing the failure of previous types of social welfare bring about the establishment of, and supposed improvement offered by, asylums. It was thanks to the power of testimony and witnessing that reforms came about for people designated as "idiots." As Steven J. Taylor points out in his book *Acts of Conscience*, reforms have closely followed exposés throughout the histories of people labeled mentally ill and mentally retarded. While Taylor's emphasis is on the lesser-known reforms initiated by conscientious objectors working in mental hospitals and training schools during World War II, the nineteenth-century reforms and exposés operated similarly. That is, the nineteenth-century poorhouse had begun as a remedy; it was considered better than the state's selling its paupers and indigent on the auction block.

Then, when poorhouses were exposed as dangerous and malevolent places, the asylum became the remedy.

Superintendent Wilbur went on to make use of the rhetorical nature of visitations, although he did so in a vastly different context than Dix. Whereas Dix exposed abuses in poorhouses as arguments for asylums, Wilbur used visitation to validate the experimental and still untrusted nature of his educational model. Superintendent Wilbur and the trustees opened up the asylum-school to endless visits from outside parties. They beckoned to visitors again and again:

> The trustees desire it to be understood, that the asylum is, at all reasonable hours, open to the inspection and examination of our citizens, but especially of the members of the Legislature and they earnestly invite the members to avail themselves of the opportunities to visit it, afforded by public carriages running every half hour from the city to Troy, passing the asylum. While their hearts will melt at the sight of mental deficiency, so hapless and miserable, a feeling of joy and hope will soon come over them, on beholding the successful application of those means of alleviating and removing the calamity which are devised by science and faith, and put in operation by time honored representatives and rulers of a people ready, always hitherto ready, to share their abundance with the children of misfortune. (2nd *Annual Report*, 41; 1st *Annual Report*, 6)

Over and over again, Wilbur touted the successes of the school, as acknowledged by those who had visited it: "No one who has visited the school will fail to recognize the subject of this description, or I think doubt the fulfillment of this prediction on my part" (2nd *Annual Report*, 173; 1st *Annual Report*, 6; 3rd *Annual Report*, 70, 82). He beckoned educators, state officials, and others to come and view the arrangements of the school and the "fitness" of its pupils. Also, the executive committee of the board of trustees, usually composed of three trustees, was scheduled to visit the asylum on the first Monday of every month "to examine into its management, inspect the condition of its pupils, audit all bills presented for payment, and decide upon the admission or dismissal of pupils" (6th *Annual Report*, 2).

By 1854, having transitioned from the small school in Albany to a larger, though still "experimental" endeavor in Syracuse, the New York State Asylum for Idiots represented the magnanimous shift in social welfare policy for which Dix had argued. The ideal of the "noble asylum" had been constructed within the idea of liberating groups of people from oppressive circumstances and relocating them to what were thought of as more suitable, and safer, settings. The failure of the poorhouse had been made public by visitations, from which had emerged scathing eyewitness accounts.

While some pupils arrived at the asylum-school from poorhouses, others came from family homes. Sometimes families and friends were able to visit the pupil and sometimes not. In light of Case No. 10 from the 1853 report, Wilbur recounts a visit from a mother:

> I cannot better illustrate this fact, than by giving an account of a visit his mother made him during the summer. When he was brought into the room to her, remembering how utterly helpless he had always been, and his probable condition when left after her death to the cold charities of the world, unfortunate and miserable, she threw her arms about his neck, and expressed a wish that he was dead. When she had become more calm, I let her see his improvement in all respects, in the school room and elsewhere; and when she left, she begged me, if there should ever be room, that I would receive her other unfortunate child, so much had her despair given place to hope, from what she had seen of improvement and promise in her child. (2nd *Annual Report*, 153–54)

Wilbur's recounting of this mother's visit was used as evidence in the 1853 Annual Report to persuade the legislators that his curriculum was bringing about much success. Another letter reprinted in the 1853 report demonstrates the desire families had to visit, and their difficulty in doing so. This letter shows how the inability to visit, as well as the distance between the pupil and his family, conjured many questions regarding the pupil's condition:

> To John's Teacher:
>
> Excuse us for we are unknown to your name. We hope you will be kind enough to answer us as soon as this reaches you, as we are very anxious to hear from John.
>
> I am a deaf mute, and I have been at school in New-York city seven years. . . . We wish to know what John does in school, and wish you to tell us about him particularly, as we love to hear from him. Tell John that he must he a good boy, and must obey you and Dr. Wilbur's commands. . . . *I expect that my father will go to Albany on a visit next spring.* Does he have a mind to learn? Tell John that my mother gives a great deal of love to him. We wish to know if he feels homesick, and does he love to learn? Please to ask if he remembers all our names, and what town we live in?

> Has John grown any since he left our home and went to school, or has his appearance changed?
>
> I must bring this to a close, as I have no more to say at present. Please tell us what your name is. We give our best love and sweet kisses to John, and give our respects to you and Dr. Wilbur. Yours with respect, Lucy G—. (2nd *Annual Report*, 163–68, Case No. 11)

This letter reveals a lot about the importance of family visits and the general feeling families might have felt for their missing sons or daughters. We do not know where John's family lived, but it can be assumed that the family only had enough money to send the father on a visit to Albany (in 1853, the school had not yet moved to Syracuse). Typically, pupils could not visit their families unless their families were able to afford the trip and the time off from work. However, by 1863 after the major reorganization of the school, it began to run on an eleven-month schedule, which meant that, as Wilbur decreed: "There shall be a vacation during the whole month of August, unless otherwise directed by the board, at which period all pupils must be removed from the Asylum by the parents or guardians, if required by the Superintendent" (12th *Annual Report*, 79). Thus, those pupils who had families would likely have returned home for a month, while those pupils without families or friends would have either returned to the poorhouse or orphanage from which they had come or stayed on at the asylum-school.[13] In addition to family visitations, students from universities often visited the asylum-school as part of their curriculum ("Inspecting an Insane Asylum," 1885). I have not found any record of visits from Syracuse University classes; however, disability studies scholar Robert Bogdan interviewed a Syracuse University alumnus and photographer who had been permitted to live at the asylum in the early part of the twentieth century in exchange for taking photographs for the institution (personal interview).

Superintendent Wilbur, in his annual reports to the legislature, repeatedly used evidence from visitations to bolster his continual claims about the school's successes, made under the assumption that funding could diminish at almost any time. This precariousness provoked Wilbur to put the school and its pupils on display in order to justify its continued existence. In every Annual Report issued during the first five years of the school (1851–55), Wilbur was forced to prove that even though experimental, the school was indispensable. Trent, in *Inventing the Feeble-Mind*, writes that it was typical of administrators such as Henry Knight, superintendent of the Connecticut Idiot Asylum, to travel to promote the institution accompanied by a few pupils who demonstrated their abilities in reading, writing, crafts, and physical exercises. Knight would also tell pupils' sad life stories (19). Wilbur's pupils performed for him, as a *New York Times* reporter observed in 1871: "It is very cheering to see the pleasure which the more intelligent of these poor creatures evince when Dr. Wilbur makes his appearance in the school-room, the dining-room, or the play-room" ("Our State Institutions"). Exhibitions were likely presented at the first meeting of the AAMO (American Association of Medical Officers, to which many asylum superintendents belonged) at the Pennsylvania Training School in Media, Pennsylvania. The second day of the meeting began with entertainment provided by the pupils and ladies of the institution: music, calisthenics, other exercises, games, and a drill by the cadets of the Pennsylvania Training School (ibid.).

Commenting on the exhibitions, Wilbur expressed concern over the continual push for display of and performance by the pupils. He wrote, "Even the witnessed or well authenticated results of efforts for their education are regarded as if they were the performances of trained animals; as if because their animal nature is developed, somewhat at the expense of the spiritual, they were endowed with instinct, instead of reason, by the Creator. But it should be remembered that they have a human origin; that however they may differ in physical, mental or moral organization they are yet human beings" (1st *Annual Report*, 56). Perhaps because of the number of people who took him up on his invitation to visit, by 1856 Wilbur was asking people to visit in small groups so that their visits would not disrupt instructional practices and "the routine of occupations and exercises of the pupils" (5th *Annual Report*, 60). He showed concern early on in respecting the interests of the pupils during visits: "I will not occupy any space in enumerating the details of modes and appliances adopted at our asylum. You have witnessed some of them in your periodical visits to the asylum, and the institution is opened by your regulations at stated periods for the inspection of all interested; nor shall I object to any still more general visiting compatible with the interests of the pupils" (1st *Annual Report*, 59). However, as time went on, Wilbur failed to show this same concern for the extent to which visits might disturb the educational program.

These widespread and orchestrated practices of visitation and display enhanced the argument that the pupils were there to be gazed upon and to perform in certain contexts for the benefit of the public face of the institution. The gaze upon and the display of pupils contained the pupil as a captive object, limited mostly to that role. This circumstantial line of thinking helped create the realm of possibility in which the institution's reputation could be improved upon by employing the visitor to act as its proponent. The visited and the displayed deploys a combination of rhetorical strategies such as witnessing and testimony to substantiate the claim that asylums were necessary and show that the asylum was doing its job to the public's liking. The tropes helped to rhetorically construct the notion of "idiocy" by situating the "idiot" as the object of someone else's gaze.

Visitations to the asylum-school by different parties and the constant exhibition or display of pupils were justified by the rhetoric that governed institutionalization, which inscribed "idiocy" as a verified fact rather than, as Foucault puts it, "an abstraction of the mind" (109). Foucault's *Birth of the Clinic: An Archaeology of Medical Perception* reveals the mechanisms at work in this type of gaze. He shows how observation and the gaze become key instruments of power and discipline: a constant gaze upon and examination of the patient or pupil creates its own logic. Foucault explains the process of nominalization that comes about through the gaze: "The hospital [asylum] domain is that in which the pathological fact appears in its singularity as an event" (109). It is the gaze—reiterated not only by doctors but by recurring and continual visitors—that constructs the "idiot."

Conclusion

The asylum-school in Syracuse was built as a segregated, isolated institution that could be visited by those who came from the "outside." In the Fourth Annual Report (1855), the trustees described their search for a secluded location that was "secured from public observation" (19). Ironically, however, observation by the public became an important tool in advocating for the asylum's success. In all of the tropes described above—*the visited and the displayed, the nameless, and the described and the counted*—a dissonance occupied the ground between that which was depicted and that which existed: the school was constructed via rhetoric as an institution of nobility so as to persuade the public of its merit: "It seems desirable . . . that attention should be paid to a pleasing exterior. This is desirable, not merely for the impression it will make upon the pupils and the friends of the pupils, but for its effect upon the public mind" (3rd *Annual Report*, 96). But the school was also a place where confinement occurred—where Goffman's "total institution" submerged identities and where Foucault's biopower corralled people constructed as abnormal and deviant. The names and individuality of the pupils were lost within mechanisms of describing and enumerating; yet, Wilbur tried desperately to create a family-like environment and an individualized curriculum, as I will discuss in the next chapter. These tropes, then, function as alternate versions of the "realities" that help construct how we think of "idiocy" and embodied difference.

In this sense, whole populations were constructed as something they may not previously have been conceived as. It was language and rhetorical processes that made them "idiots." The designation of "idiocy" did something to people that otherwise would not have been done without these complex lines of arguments and tropes. And the public responded accordingly. Arguments coalesced into tropes, which transformed public understanding. Certain types of physical and behavioral descriptions, enumeration, anonymity, visitation, and the display of "idiots" became commonplace. Yet, it was Wilbur himself who recognized "idiocy" as a "stamp . . . [that] has been set by an erroneous public opinion" (2nd *Annual Report*, 59). But one man could not control the meaning that had been unleashed. The tropes constituted a discursive transformation of the construct of "idiocy," which, once transformed by language, was thought to be solid, stable. These practices all comprised dominant rhetorics of disability in that the practices entailed symbolic strategies that were enmeshed mostly in compliance with cultural logics that differentiated between a normal and an abnormal. The tropes of *the described and the counted, the nameless, the visited, and the displayed* all epitomized cultural logics of normativity that attempted to "reform" people who fell outside the "normal" range. These tropes were the signifiers that determined how we think of "idiocy" and embodied difference.

"Idiocy" is metaphoric, not in the sense that it should stand in to teach a particular lesson (like the trope of the blind man who is ignorant) but rather that it is constituted by myth, narrative, and constructed truths, rather than by "real" biological difference. Tropes are constructed realities; they are language that displaces people in particularly complex ways and yet they are the meanings by which we seem to abide most. The arguments constructed by educators and reformers shift people's identities away from who they may have been before. The public arguments that reformers and educators made in the nineteenth century constructed realities that had material effects on real people; the asylum-school in Syracuse demonstrates this succinctly. And finally: Can we know a nineteenth-century pupil of the asylum-school beyond these arguments and the tropes that epitomize them? Why must we at least try? In the following chapter, I explain how the asylum and its staff continued to use rhetoric in an attempt to retrofit their pupils, once they were admitted, into the more "ordinary."

CHAPTER 3

In Pursuit of the Active Life

The Roots, Rhetoric, and Recursiveness of "Special" (All) Education

> Touch comes before sight, before speech. It is the first language and the last, and it always tells the truth.
>
> —Margaret Atwood, *The Blind Assassin*

> [A]n individual is nothing fixed, given ready-made. It is something achieved, and achieved not in isolation but with the aid and support of conditions, cultural and physical.
>
> —John Dewey, "The Future of Liberalism"

All education is in some way ideological and in some way "special"; every curriculum emphasizes some things over others. Nineteenth-century "idiot education" was quintessentially ideological in its interest in the body, sensation, experience, social and civic relations, its pragmatism, and its individualized approach.[1] Learning—be it linguistic, occupational, even mathematical—was always corporeal. The educational curriculum of the asylum-school attempted to mold the pupil via codified practices of what was called "sensationalism": knowledge was integrated into the mind via the senses. Nothing could be known without sense experience. Most importantly, not only does this philosophy of education lie at the root of "special"[2] education but liberal humanist education in a broad sense has borrowed its corporeal, sensorial, experiential, and utilitarian nature. But while today the term *special education* is viewed as a subcategory under general education—an applied specialization within it—the curriculum at the asylum-school was indeed a model for *all* education. As Simi Linton argues in *Claiming Disability: Knowledge and Identity*, rather than seeing the two knowledge bases as separate, we need a "broad based epistemology of inclusion, a knowledge base grounded in the liberal arts that provides tools that academics and civilians need to make critical social, intellectual, and professional changes" (81). General education can glean from this asylum-school curriculum by integrating general approaches with "special" approaches. As Linton points out, disability then can be viewed as a variable method or approach to the education of all students rather than a pathologized and separate curriculum that sets disabled people apart (82).

In this chapter, I demonstrate how nuances of the curriculum might inform general approaches. I piece together the curriculum—known as Physiological Education—as it was theorized by French special educator Edouard Seguin, and as it was put into practice at the asylum-school by Superintendent H. B. Wilbur. Bodily, intellectual, social, and civic modification happens in the context of schooling. The asylum-school worked to create a second, seemingly improved nature (what is known as phusiopoesis) in its pupils—through rigorous pedagogical and rehabilitative methods, the asylum-school attempted to overhaul the physical qualities that affect the social, civic, intellectual, vocational, and moral aspects of the pupil. Whereas in chapter 2 I developed a theory of resignification that occurs through metaphor, this chapter focuses on the ways an education that emphasizes the senses and the body can be both limiting and transformative. Despite the curriculum's emphasis on creating a second nature, the reality was that it offered only a very limited version of becoming to its pupils by today's standards, though it offered a progressive education by the standards of its own time. This limitation invites critique, while at the same time its progressive nature and its importance as a predecessor to experiential education demands recognition.

The Roots of "Special" Education

On September 8, 1854 at the asylum's opening ceremony, the Reverend Samuel J. May[3] spoke in utter adulation of Edouard Seguin, who is credited with systematizing one of the first curricula for what we now think of as "special education"[4] (1st *Annual Report*, 57). Reverend May extolled Seguin and his colleagues:

> They were the first to conceive . . . that *idiots can be educated*. And here we have with us, in our very midst, the man—the Frenchman—to whom, under God, the subjects of this terrible malady; their relatives, the communities in which they were born, and our

> common humanity owe more, perhaps, than to any other individual. He is entitled to an expression of our respect and gratitude. Let the name of Edward Seguin never be forgotten. (4th *Annual Report*, 220; emphasis added)

Edouard Seguin (1812–1880), a French-born physician and educator, studied under Jean Marc Gaspard Itard, who had been the first to write about his pedagogy specifically designed for those considered to have deficient mental capacity (Itard worked fairly unsuccessfully with "The Wild Child," aka Victor, of Aveyron). Seguin began teaching in 1841 at Salpêtrière, the Hospital for Incurables in Paris, where ten of his pupils showed success, and the next year transferred to Bicêtre to work closely with Itard. Bicêtre was the asylum in Paris where Phillipe Pinel had instituted a revolutionary method called "moral treatment," which aimed to treat the insane humanely. At Bicêtre, Seguin worked closely with Itard but eventually deemed his method too limited (Talbot, 55). While many in Paris, including Itard and Jean-Étienne Dominique Esquirol, another proponent of moral treatment, had thought "idiocy" was incurable or untreatable, Seguin set about proving them wrong, and was subsequently recognized by the Academy of Sciences Medical Committee in Paris, who declared that he had in fact found a way to educate "idiots" (Talbot, 59–60). In 1848, Seguin emigrated to the United States, and while it is unclear exactly why, it has been said that he left France because of accusations of mistreating children at Bicêtre (Trent, 40). He then practiced as a physician in Ohio, before moving in 1863 to New York City to practice his method of educating "idiots" at the Randall's Island Asylum. Seguin would become the heaviest influence on Hervey Backus Wilbur, superintendent of the New York State Asylum for Idiots, having frequently set up study and practice at Wilbur's asylum in Syracuse.

Seguin's highly regarded work was not an isolated theory separate from conventional philosophies of the time; rather, its was an amalgam of Enlightenment and post-Enlightenment priciples that connected theories of the mind and ways of learning and knowing to ideas of universal education. Rather than separate and unrelated, "special" education in its infancy in the United States was already connected to general theories of the time. Seguin argued that the "idiot" could learn via systematic training that persuaded the will of the pupil to act. His pedagogy centered specifically around what he called the "trinitarian hypothesis"—cultivating *activity*, *intelligence*, and the *will*. Seguin explained the trinity thus:

> Our method [Physiological Education], to be really physiological, must adapt itself in principles as well as in its means and instruments, to the healthy development and usage of the functions, particularly of those of the life of relation. . . . Man being a unit, is artificially

> analyzed, for study's sake, into his three prominent vital expressions: *activity*, *intelligence*, and *will*. We consider the idiot as a man infirm in the expressions of his trinity; and we understand the method of training idiots, *or* mankind, as the philosophical agency by which the unity of manhood can be reached as far as practicable in our day, through the trinary analysis. (*Idiocy: Its Diagnosis*, 171)

The three divisions were not antagonistic nor were they mutually exclusive; rather, they worked together, Seguin explained, toward a "harmonious training" of the whole person. "Physiological education" worked toward a "harmonious training of the whole child" by restoring the three functions so that the pupil seemingly isolated because of faulty function could enter into "the common life" (228, 172). This point is important because it demonstrates how Seguin's trinity worked to promote the pupil's entry into a social life of relations and associations wherein the pupil could engage in "ordinary" endeavors. This "integration" into civic life required a complex system of becoming that included physical, moral, intellectual, and vocational transformation.

To further understand the curriculum, we can trace the roots of Seguin's method to a range of educational and philosophical movements that aimed to educate the whole person via the senses. As documented in his philosophical tracts, Seguin tells how he was influenced by sensationalism, alienism (early psychiatry), moral treatment, the object method of instruction, experimental psychology (philosophy of the mind), and education of the deaf. He places his work in conversation with John Locke's identification of sensation as the entry-point for learning, Etienne de Condilllac's theories that directly link sensation to ideas, Jacob Rodriguez Pereire's use of oral training of the deaf, Philippe Pinel's moral treatment method, which emphasized benevolence over cruelty (originally in the "rehabilitation" of the insane), Jean-Marc Gaspard Itard's individualized teaching of the Wild Boy of Aveyron, and Johann Pestalozzi's theories of an experiential, object-focused, and scaffolded education.

Seguin's "special education" curriculum should not be seen as a marginal theory serviceable only in specialized settings. Rather, his work, as Mabel Talbot argues in her 1964 study of Seguin (one of very few works about Seguin translated into English), should be recognized as having been integrated back into mainstream educational practices and used as the foundation for nuanced methods such as, for example, Montessori's method. Part of the importance of recovering Seguin's method is to explore the impact his experiential, physiological, and object-oriented pedagogy has had on all education.

Superintendent Wilbur sought to apply Seguin's physiological education to his management of the asylum in Syracuse. Both men aimed to create "harmony" for the whole pupil. At the opening ceremony of the asylum-school in 1854, Wilbur confirmed his utter gratitude for Seguin's work, much of which had been researched and applied at the asylum in Syracuse by Seguin himself. In 1844, Seguin had published his first book, *Traitement Moral.* The book was *the* most important influence on Wilbur's pedagogy (Graney, 5). In 1852, Seguin introduced his method of Physiological Education, as outlined in *Traitement Moral,* at Samuel G. Howe's school in South Boston (where Helen Keller studied), which had opened a small section for the education of "idiots" within its school for the blind (Talbot, 68; Trent, 43). But Seguin didn't stay long at Howe's school and, after Boston, spent considerable time at Syracuse until 1866 (4th *Annual Report*, 57; 5th *Annual Report*, 15; Talbot, 77). Seguin's *Idiocy and Its Treatment by the Physiological Method* (1866) was an updated version of the first book, except that this book was based on his close study with Wilbur at Syracuse; in fact, the book venerates Syracuse for successfully carrying out Seguin's trinitarian hypothesis. Published in 1864, *Idiocy: Its Diagnosis and Treatment by the Psychological Method* reflects Seguin's formidable presence at the asylum-school, as he frequently prescribes a particular practice in the text, then refers to its application by Wilbur at Syracuse (*Idiocy: Its Diagnosis*, 405, 476).

Wilbur had started what is thought of as the first school for "idiots" in the United States in Barre, Massachusetts, in 1848, and then had been recruited to run the New York State Asylum, first in Albany and then Syracuse in 1854. As Seguin did in his sometimes allied, sometimes contested relationship to the work of his educational predecessors, Wilbur both heavily aligned himself with Seguin's Physiological Method and diverged from it. Wilbur, in fact, followed Seguin's trinitiarian hypothesis, as seen by his defining "idiocy" as "the want of a natural or harmonious development of the *mental, active, and moral powers* of a human being" (1st *Annual Review*, 49; italics added). Like Seguin, Wilbur was concerned with harmonizing activity, intellect, and the will through educational discipline meant to transfigure the "idiot" into a "human shape." Wilbur was invested in providing an education that gave people opportunities to be a part of civil society.

All Sensations Are Touch, All Ideas Are Sensations

> 1st. Infirm in mobility and sensibility.
>
> —Seguin, "Origin and the Treatment and Training of Idiots"

Sensation that roused *activity* was "the *prolegomena* of the treatment of idiots." Sensation brought the "idiot" out of isolation and into the world of relations and associations (Seguin, "Origin," 29). The curricular precept of *activity* moved the student from physical and social isolation toward relation to and harmony with the world. This happened by awakening the senses, muscles, and nerves.

The day to day routine in the school was characterized by constant physical activity and movement, because it was thought that the sensations and will could be awakened further through habit, reiteration, and constant activity. In the early life of the institution (1854–1860), when between thirty and seventy students lived within its walls, the pupils adhered to a strict schedule in which every moment was taken up with activity and learning. The pupils awoke at dawn. In the small dorm rooms (where boys and girls were separated), attendants taught less able pupils to work buttons through holes, tie shoes, and push their arms through shirtsleeves. The more abled pupils assisted the less abled. Those who could walk unassisted walked outdoors to get their blood flowing, or, if weather did not permit outdoor exercise, performed calisthenics in the gymnasium. Everyone gathered for breakfast in the family-style dining room. After breakfast, which some had helped prepare, the older pupils made beds, swept, and cleaned. All students engaged in as much physical activity as possible until school began at nine o'clock in the Sensation Room.

This constant motion typified the first aspect of Seguin's trinitarian hypothesis of *activity* as an awakening and development of sensation, which was combined with development of the muscular and nervous system. Seguin's theory of sensation was drawn, while it also diverged, from the sensationalism of Locke and Condillac. More than a century and a half prior to Seguin's work, Locke had posited that all ideas emerge from experience that is grounded in sense impression. For Locke, knowledge arises first out of sensation and then reflection (*Essay*, 104–105). Sense impressions, followed by reflection, are the raw materials that form ideas. Seguin derived his methods from these notions of the development of knowledge as he also drew from Locke's concept of the tabula rasa: the mind is an empty, permeable slate at birth. As experience arrives via sensation, the mind becomes furnished with ideas. The tabula rasa was a fundamental notion for Seguin in the education of "idiots" because, he reasoned, if all people are born with a blank slate, including the "idiot," then all have the capacity to inscribe the blank slate with knowledge. At the asylum-school, it was thought that the blank slate could best be filled by first awakening the senses, muscles, and nerves.

Edward Corbett, in exploring Locke's contribution to education, illuminates how Locke's theories of sensation have influenced theory and pedagogy. This helps us better understand why it was considered important to educate or "awaken" the senses in the asylum-school. Corbett points to the contemporary students' "narrowly circumscribed range of . . . experiences," which he then further explains through Locke (426). Corbett looks at a passage from Locke that proposes that if a child were isolated from certain experiences, for example the experience of certain colors such as scarlet or green, then the child would have no idea of those colors as an adult. Corbett suggests a way to increase exposure to experiences: teachers should "expose [students] to situations which can expand their reservoir of ideas, either by providing new sense perceptions or by encouraging mental reflections" (ibid.). These concepts of Locke's, illuminated by Corbett, were foundational for Seguin's theory that sense impressions were the gateway into the mind. The senses could only be stimulated if the range of experience was increased.

While Locke influenced Seguin with his theories of sensation, experience, and the tabula rasa, Étienne de Condillac influenced Seguin by pointing even more emphatically to the importance of sensation in learning. Condillac is known for having brought to France Locke's notion that knowledge comes from both sensation and reflection. In *Edouard Seguin*, Mabel E. Talbot describes Condillac's theory of sensation as expressed in his work *Treatise on Sensations*: she writes that his goal was "to develop [the sensitivity] by all possible means, and to prepare the mind for attention by making the senses ready to receive more vivid impressions" (24). Most of all, however, Condillac veered from Locke by hypothesizing that all knowledge was sensation only. Therefore, sensation was more than just the source of all knowledge; ideas *were* sensations transformed into ideas (Carr, xxii; Condillac, 236). Ideas, including memory and imagination, are all a form of sensation, according to Condillac.

Condillac's hypothesis was important to Seguin because Seguin's teacher, Jean-Marc Gaspard Itard—the educator of the deaf who tried to "civilize" Victor, the Wild Boy of Aveyron—had utilized Condillac's theory of sensation in attempting to teach Victor. Itard eventually gave up trying to educate Victor using theories of sensation; Itard considered Victor uneducable, and Victor spent the rest of his life at Bicêtre, an asylum in Paris. Seguin developed his own pedagogy for the education of "idiots" at Bicêtre, the School for Deaf-Mutes in Paris, where Victor remained. There, Seguin posited that Itard had not been wrong in the method he'd used trying to educate Victor, but that, rather, his methods had been incomplete (*Idiocy: Its Diagnosis*, 65; "Origin," 10; Talbot, 57). Seguin explained the unfinished nature of Itard's work: "[Itard] obstinately saw in the idiot the savage; and, resting in his studies, as well as in his faith, on the materialistic doctrines of Locke and Condillac, his teachings sometimes reached the senses of his pupil, but never penetrated to his mind and soul" ("Origin," 7). Seguin's lifework, then, was to correct Itard's theories: he began with sensation, as Itard had, but then went much farther in the direction of intellectual training. In addition to this major modification, another important deviation from Itard's sensationalist theory was that while Itard initiated education of the senses first with hearing and sight and then with touch, Seguin believed education of the senses began with touch and proceeded to sight, hearing, taste, and smell (*Idiocy: Its Diagnosis*, 345; Itard, 55). According to Seguin, then, touch was the sensation most primary in creating interconnection with others.

Touch, in the trinitarian hypothesis, was indeed the primary sense of which all other senses were a manifestation (*Idiocy: Its Diagnosis*, 52, 305). In addition to gleaning from Itard's mistakes, Seguin derived his commitment to the primacy of tactility from Jacob Rodriguez Pereire (1715–1780), a member of the Royal Society of London and an educator of the deaf who was the subject of an 1846 biography written by Seguin himself. The fact that Seguin wrote Pereire's biography demonstrates the level of influence Pereire had on Seguin. Pereire had expanded upon Juan Pablo Bonet's manual alphabet (what we now know as sign language) and, more important to the discussion of tactility, was thought to be one of the first educators, if not the first, to orally teach deaf students to speak.[5] His oral method worked through touch and vibration. Students would feel the mouth of the teacher as well as their own mouths in order to mimic the position of the tongue and lips and gauge the force of the release of air from the mouth during verbal articulation (*Idiocy: Its Diagnosis*, 51–52). Seguin writes of Pereire's declamation of the importance of tactility, "Hence, a given vibration producing only a given sound, the deaf taught to perceive the vibration, could not imitate it without reproducing likewise the corresponding sound of language. It is thus that [Pereire] practically made his pupils hear through the skin, and utter exactly what they so heard. By this discovery, Pereire demonstrated to the physiologists of his day, that all the senses are modifications of the tact, all touch of some sort" (*Idiocy: Its Diagnosis*, 52). Not only would use of the sense of touch become the entryway into education of the senses and the focus of *activity*, but also it was the principle Seguin used to teach both deaf and hearing pupils to speak, as will be discussed later in the chapter.

The Object Method, the Hand, and the Garden System

As further means to educate the senses and create relation and interconnectedness, Seguin adapted the Swiss educator Johann Pestalozzi's methods, which included the object method. The object method gave the curriculum an experiential and palpable aim; by using objects, pupils touched, felt, and saw in order to learn. In 1801, after Pestalozzi transformed his farm in Switzerland into a school for orphans, he wrote *How Gertrude Taught Her Children*, his pedagogical treatise, which locates learning first in observation and second in consciousness and speech. He did not advocate rote memorization; rather, his pedagogy was centered around the notion that each pupil could uniquely develop her own nature by observing real objects in the world. Instruction, he believed, should be modified to fit each pupil. Similarly, for Seguin, even math and grammar started with bodily and sensory processes and experience; everything was learned through things and learned in relation to what was around the pupil. Wilbur and Seguin believed in the power of *things* as a crucial mode of learning. Pestalozzi's philosophy has been discussed in detail by Lucille Schultz. In her book *The Young Composers: Composition's Beginnings in Nineteenth-Century Schools*, Schultz argues that the history of writing instruction is indebted to Pestalozzi's experiential object instruction, which, long before people such as Elbow, Murray, and Rose advocated experiential and expressivist pedagogy, had an effect on the way students composed (Schultz, 6, 79).

During Wilbur's time, a method of experiential education known as the Oswego System of Object Instruction, which drew its method from Pestalozzi, became popular as *the* method that informed experiential education. The Object Method began with sensation or *activity* and proceeded to the *intellect*:

1. Activity is the law of childhood. Get the pupil to do—educate the hand.
2. Cultivate the faculties in their natural order—transform the mind, then furnish it.
3. Cultivate the senses and never tell a child what he can discover for himself.
4. Reduce every subject to its elements—one difficulty at a time is enough.
5. Proceed step by step.
6. Develop the idea, then give the term—cultivate language. Ideas should precede language.
7. Proceed from the known to the unknown.
8. First synthesize, then analyze—not the order of the subject, but the order of nature. (Wilbur, "Object")

Wilbur agreed with the Oswego System's initiation of education at the level of the hand (no. 1), its cultivating the faculties (speech, memory, imitation, etc.) (no. 2), its relying upon the senses and self-discovery (no. 3), and its moving methodically (nos. 4 and 5); however, Wilbur's harshest critique of the system came in response to no. 6 ("Develop the idea, then give the term, cultivate language—ideas should precede language"). Wilbur commented that no. 6 was "one of the most vicious methods of the Oswego System" ("Object," 196). He explained that observation should be kept entirely separate from language until language developed naturally; it should not be forced. Language should develop naturally as the desires of the individual increased: create the material need and the communicative need would follow (ibid.). Pupils first utilized complex observational powers using only the senses; they discriminated, compared, reasoned, judged, decided, and willed utilizing the senses and "without the use of any language!" ("Object," 197). Rather than through language, intellectual power was nurtured first through movement and bodily sensation.

In this denunciation of the Oswego System's premature use of language, Wilbur placed heavy emphasis on the powers of the object and the powers of observation over the use of language. He was not against the use of language, obviously, but rather, by isolating observation and emphasizing the use of sensation, he attempted to avoid applying language to objects and experiences in a rote manner. In aligning himself with Condillac, Locke, and Seguin, he aimed to draw ideas (and thus language) directly from sensation. However, sensation and experience had to be fully realized before language could be deployed—and, language at times could obstruct "correct" development by forgoing the senses and thereby not allowing the mind to learn along with the body.

Despite Wilbur's criticisms of the Oswego System, he adhered to the method of object instruction that educated the senses in order to foster control over the muscular system, awaken the imitative faculty, and focus attention in preparation for study (1st *Annual Report*, 17). Colors, for example, were taught in the Sensation Room by darkening the room to display the colored windowpanes and use them as objects of learning; cards, fruit, ribbons, balls, marbles, and other colored objects were also used (*Idiocy: Its Diagnosis*, 376). A color was learned by attending to real objects that had functional purposes—windows that altered the light or marbles that made sense in the context of a game. The senses were educated using objects in the context of their functional natures until the student's sense perception performed with "correctness, precision and celerity" (ibid., 18). Mathematics was taught by Wilbur with grapes, pears, marbles, nuts, etc. Training relied upon an endless supply of material things.

This use of real objects began with training in prehension (to seize, hold, and let go, or to take, keep, and lose hold) (*Idiocy: Its Diagnosis*, 252). The object method opened sense impressions by working only with those things that could be first touched, felt, or used by the hand. The hand was seen as the main instrument that willed the pupil to action, for "the hand is the best servant of man; the best instrument of work; the best translator of thoughts; the most skillful hand is yet, in respect to certain realizations, as it were idiotic; our own hand shrivels before we suspect the thousands of ideas which it might realize" (3rd *Annual Report,* 29; *Idiocy,* 261). A pupil learned to extend the arm, open the hand, and grasp ("Treatment of an Idiotic Hand"). Other lessons in the Sensation Room included learning names and functions of the "different parts of a door, as the lock, the handle, the bolt, and key"; pupils learned how these objects worked by using them (2nd *Annual Report,* 145). The hand was run over different surfaces and immersed in warm and cold liquids to stimulate sensation; and it was considered better to do all of this training within some sort of useful or functional occupation such as washing hands, opening windows, etc. Coordination and willed movement of both the hand and arm, as well as controlled movements of the head and eyes were to be achieved before the legs and feet were trained to walk. In addition to controlled movement, willed immobility was also imposed, in which pupils were meant to still those movements that were seemingly not under their control. Arms and other body parts were held in place by restraints. All of these physical actions were meant to bring the body under control.

Due to the experiential nature of the pedagogy and the extensive attempt to attend to the body, Seguin's pedagogy was known as a "garden-system" of training where, as Talbot notes, those who could walk or dig or lift objects would learn outdoors (Talbot, 79). Pupils used their hands to collect natural objects from the outdoors. Classes were held outdoors whenever possible (*Idiocy: Its Diagnosis,* 502). In this sense, Seguin and Wilbur's pedagogies were based on the concrete and pragmatic. They believed in experience and sensation rather than lecturing or recitation or anything that was considered beyond direct understanding. Seguin exclaims: "Away, then, with books! Give us the Assyrian and Jewish mode of instruction. The representative signs of thought where painted, engraved, sculptured in deepness or in relief sensible to the eye and to the touch; the tables of the mosaic laws appear in the midst of thunder and of the lightning's flash" (Seguin, "Origin," 33).

The Face, the Posture, Walking, Then Thinking

As the pupil underwent various experiences, the body was coaxed into transformation. Physical exercise occurred in the gymnasium, an important detached building thirty-five by sixty feet in size (4th *Annual Review,* 118). Much attention had been paid in the annual reports to the gymnasium, as the edifice was said to be the equal of those in the common schools (5th *Annual Review,* 72). The gymnasium's purpose was to "develop muscular power, dexterity and a proper carriage" (24th *Annual Review*, 90). To reshape the physique, attention was paid to both deportment and countenance. It was thought that training and rehabilitation in these areas would make the pupil physically stronger, more able, and more physically pleasing, which in turn, it was thought, would create someone who could enter into civic endeavors as a fit citizen. A pupil's physical state was conceived as dreadful. Case no. 12, A. M., a boy eight years old and of usual size, was prepared for necessary training to counter the observation that "his countenance betrayed his 'idiocy'" (15th *Annual Review*). Another pupil's tongue "protruded from his mouth, and his chin and dress were wet with saliva. . . . [W]hen he left, he was neat, good looking and well behaved" (6th *Annual Review*, 25).

Besides attention to the face, posture straightening was enforced. Sitting and standing up straight would have to be achieved before the pupil was taught to walk. The "Backboard" did just the trick: the Backboard corrected "shoulders rounded by dejection, crooked sternums, concave clavicles, narrow chests, vicious structures . . . curved spines, inequality of strength and structure of the two sides of the body" (*Idiocy: Its Diagnosis*, 267–68). The board was propped against a wall. The student lay on his back against the board. He raised his arms to grab hold of the pegs in the board above him and tried to keep his body stationary by stepping on the pegs below. Then he attempted to ascend along the pegs until he reached the top of the board. Seguin observed that "[t]here he is allowed a little rest, as well to repose himself as to appreciate the novel mode of ascension, the distance from the soil, the look of everything seen for the first time from so high, and to be refreshed from past emotions, so that he can stand what will come next" (ibid.). Upon descending, the pupil's spine was aligned by helpers on a vertical line so that "the most shocking difference between shoulders, deviations, already sensible of the spine, shortness of one limb, disappear under the uniform action of this equalizer, the Backboard" (ibid).

The gymnasium further educated the senses and the body through a multitude of activities that included calisthenics, military-style drills and marching, physical exercises, muscular strengthening and manipulation, and mobility and bodily training. The gym was filled with equipment: a treadmill, dumbbells, balancing poles, a pulley swing with springboard, ladders, inclined backboard with pegged handholds to correct posture. While the Sensation Room educated at the base level of touch, taste, smell, hearing, and sight, the gymnasium was the place where the actual physique and physical shape of the pupil were remade.

Other important physical exercises included walking, which was considered close to godliness. Walking was learned after correct posture was attained. Stairs were climbed and the feeling of walking was simulated by handholds and extra support. In learning to walk correctly, pupils would have to navigate rough terrain and traverse obstacle courses: one activity directed pupils to enter the small space of a room, or an outdoor space (depending on the weather) that had been transformed into an obstacle course consisting of

> shaded turf, of all the planes, horizontal, inclined in the four directions, abruptly cut, rough, stony, slippery, narrow, etc., which could present themselves as ordinary impediments to regular progression. The child must go through these difficulties with or without dumb-bells, steadily commanded, or urged by the excitement of music. . . . The act of directing each foot on each form is one of the best exercises for limbs which have previously escaped all control; but what a superior exercise it is for the head above, which has never suspected its regulating power: to walk among so many difficulties is to think. (*Idiocy: Its Diagnosis*, 245–46)

"Correct" facial expression, posture, and staying upright and walking were all thought to incite intellectual activity and to prepare the pupil for advanced mental operations (1st *Annual Review*, 57).

Physical improvement on the muscular level also translated to preparation of boys for military duty. Military service for boys was viewed as extremely successful in that it validated their ability to participate in civic endeavors. Seguin observes,

> Thus, with taste and show, are exhibited hoops, skates, sleds, balloons, ten-pins, kites, wooden and other balls, all arranged against the walls in attractive symmetry. Bows and arrows, wooden swords and guns, occupy in rows accessible positions, ready to be seized by the children, who need to learn the use of war implements; the determined attitude, the quick step, the firm grasp, the sure aim, etc. Even the fighting value of this military training in so feeble hands can be no longer despised, since two of the pupils of the New York State Institution went into the army of the Union, understanding very well what they fought for; one died of the fatigues of the campaigns; the other, wounded in two battles under Sheridan, died at Winchester. (*Idiocy: Its Diagnosis*, 534)

The curriculum became pragmatic, for example, as it did during a time of war. Yet, Wilbur and Seguin both were careful not to overemphasize activity in the gymnasium. They did not wish to be like the "Grecians," who overcultivated the body; nor did they wish to be like the Sophists who overcultivated the intellect (*Idiocy: Its Diagnosis*, 227). Through this training of the senses, the "idiot" whose mind had begun as a tabula rasa in complete isolation was now able to will the body to act. The pupil then was ready for the supreme goal of education of the intellect: "The glorious effulgence of the light, the gloomy shadows of the darkness, the striking contrasts of colors, the infinite variety of form, the smoothness or hardness of substances, the sounds and the pauses of music, the eloquent harmonies of human gesture, look and speech, these are the powerful agents of their transition from physiological to mental education" (Seguin, "Origin," 32). As sensation and physical mobility were trained, the student entered into ideas, judgments, and decision making. Yet sensory, nervous, and muscular training was also inseparable from reflective and mental training. And, physical training continued to constitute a "corresponding culture" to mental training and vice versa (ibid.,194).

Sensations, Notions, Then Ideas

> 2d. Infirm in perception and reasoning.
>
> —"Origin and the Treatment and Training of Idiots"

Sensation was only a starting point for development. While physical acts of willed movement formed the foundation for training in *activity*, it was the reflective intellectual act that brought the "idiot" even closer to "the common life." Specifically, intellectual training included education in imitation, speech, language, writing, reading, arithmetic, and geography. The trinitarian hypothesis connected sensation with intellectual processes, and no previous learning was lost. Pupils acted on both the sensorial and intellectual level throughout the training; both sensation and intellect were continually linked through an ongoing "apparatus of action" (*Idiocy: Its Diagnosis*, 192). For Seguin, reflective capability existed in all minds; it began with sensation but was perfected through training of the intellect.

By returning here to a brief discussion of Seguin's sensationalism, we can understand how he transitioned from training the senses to training the intellect. Seguin posited what he called the *functional circle*, which situates notions between sensations and ideas. James Trent, in his discussion of Seguin, offers an important analysis of the untranslated *Hygiene and Education* (1843), which explains how Seguin deviated from his predecessors' (Itard, Condillac, and Locke) notions that ideas emerged directly out of sense experience. Rather than sensation being directly linked to ideas, Seguin theorized that the *notion* mediated between sensation and idea (Trent, 48; *Idiocy: Its Diagnosis*, 436). In the idea of the notion lay the emergence of reflective intellectual acts. Seguin theorized that "[p]erceptions are acquired by the mind through the senses, not by the senses. . . . To facilitate the study, we distinguished the notions from the ideas as if they were two products of different functions" (*Idiocy: Its Diagnosis*, 436).

Notions that Seguin taught included but are not limited to the notions of distance, purpose, a plane, force, and space. A notion was formed through sensation, which then led to an idea. For example, through touch and visuality, a pupil experienced a flower vase that rested on a table. Next, the vase was acknowledged through the notions of space and purpose—the vase sits atop the table and is filled with flowers in order to perhaps conjure aesthetic pleasure. From an understanding of the notion of the vase, the pupil was taught the idea of the vase, or, that the object was a *vase*. The pupil learned along the continuum from sensation to notion (distance, purpose, plane, force, space) to idea, so that he or she moved from the substantial and corporeal to the functional and then to the rational and intellectual. Notions mediated between the physiological world and the intellectual world. In this sense, for Seguin, ideas were not directly linked to sensation (as Itard, Condillac, and Locke had theorized), nor were ideas entirely separate from sensation (as Descartes had theorized). Seguin's use of the *notion* as a mediation modified sensationalist philosophy by adding the important procedural step of function and purpose to the learning process. This was crucial to his education of the intellect.

Imitation as Social Relation

Also crucial to training of the intellect was skillfulness in imitation. Though imitation was a main component of all aspects of physiological education, it appears to have been most central in training the intellect and in learning to speak, write, and read. Seguin invoked Herbert Spenser's prescription of imitation as a sound educational practice and he attempted to be careful to not confuse imitation with rote practice (*Idiocy: Its Diagnosis*, 71). Imitation, rather than a rote practice, is a core intellectual faculty that has important functions. Seguin described imitation as "the sudden, unexpected call into action of any organ that can be moved by the will. . . . [It is] the broad ground of our training in education" (ibid. 296). He divided imitation into personal and objective types. *Personal imitation* referred to actions limited to the functions of the body while *objective imitation* extended beyond the body to include actions that affected relations and determined perception of the properties of objects (ibid., 292, 302). Objective imitation that moved thinking outside the individual's body (and which follows alongside object education) used objects to generate intellectual acts. An example included the teacher "showing," not commanding or directing, the pupil to place objects on a table in a particular way. Seguin explained that the intellectual act developed from objective imitation: the student mimicked the teacher's placement of objects on the table "till the exercise of simple imitation becomes quite intellectual, requiring at least a good deal of attention and power of combination. Later, the [teacher] creates combinations of two or more blocks at once, and the [student] must imitate all of it at once; and finally the [teacher] creates a combination of a few blocks, destroys it, and orders the [student] to build up the like, whose pattern he now can find only in his mind" (ibid., 378).

This type of exercise, along with the majority of other imitation techniques used, was not considered rote or mechanistic; Seguin concurred with Pestalozzi's disavowal of rote memorization. For Seguin, rote obstructed progress. Seguin stipulates that "[b]etter one thing thoroughly known than a hundred remembered. Teaching so many facts is not so fruitful as teaching how to find the relations between a single one and its natural properties and connexions . . . what enters the mind alone, dies in it alone" (*Idiocy: Its Diagnosis*, 195–96, 211). Rather than simply remembering the shape of a letter in the alphabet, for example, the pupil also learned, as explained, the notion and idea of a letter. While use of memory was prescribed only provisionally by Seguin, imitation practices were widely utilized. But because Seguin let his reader know he was aware of the iconic image of the "village idiot" as an imitator, his pedagogy approached imitation cautiously. Imitation was used to develop spontaneity in action and relationship with others; the teacher had to be careful not to induce "monomania" or to forgo knowledge for memory. Seguin warned teachers to teach *memotechny* (the art of memory) by, for example in teaching reading, allowing the memory of the student to connect the ideas and names of letters to their forms (the notion of a letter) rather than memorizing their location on a letter board (ibid., 396). Imitation was rhetorical in that it was not practiced as unmeaning gesture but rather had some sort of social and contextual meaning "which can produce work at any time" ("Origin," 28).

These uses of memory as connected to experience and observation, rather than rote memorization, reflected progressive practices current at the time, wherein, as Lucille Schultz and David Gold point out, the experiential education of Johann Pestalozzi translated well to and became an important part of a rhetorical education (*Young Composers*; *Rhetoric at the Margins*). In *The Methodical Memory*, Sharon Crowley also discusses how memory was used for writing in the mode of description that drew most heavily from the student's sensory observations.

Seguin intended his pedagogy to be one of action, interconnectedness, and relation; this was true also of his use of imitation. Ideally, simple imitation became intellectual through the process of creating social relation (*Idiocy: Its Diagnosis*, 378). Imitation was seen as the effect one person had upon another—or, how susceptible people were to influence. The initial practices of imitation involved the student's concentration and connection with the teacher, which then evolved into group practices. And, when engaging in imitation practices, whether individually or in groups, the pupil was taught to connect the part to the whole, the individual to the group, and to perceive the context of objects and ideas. Seguin taught how, through relationship and context, people and things were interconnected and associated. According to Seguin, when a geometrical point was taught, for example, this *pedagogy of association* "must not make us forgetful of the line to which this point belongs; the line, of the body it limits; the body, of its accessory properties; the properties, of the possible associations of the subject under consideration, with its surroundings: an idea is not an isolated image of one thing, but the representation in a unit of all the facts related to the imaged object" (*Idiocy and Its Treatment*, 197).

Speech, Language, Listening, and Recitation

In addition to this use of imitation that was meant to conjure the intellect and move the pupil into social relation, the student was expected to have speech if he or she was to enter into common life. While speech was considered as part of the training of the intellect, it was practiced in relation to physiology. Wilbur viewed speech as "exclusively a human faculty," while language was conceived as "both the means and instrument of thought" ("Relation," 7–8). For Wilbur, speech was the physiological mechanism, while language expressed the relationships between objects and ideas; speech was physiological, oral language was intellectual and reflective (8). While effective language use was an ideal in the curriculum, speech teaching tended to overshadow the rhetorical and intellectual uses of language. The curriculum here necessitated attention to those more fundamental aspects of communication, oftentimes at the neglect of more nuanced teaching of the rhetoricity and complexity of language.

Seguin theorized the teaching of speech in three ways: one, in the schoolroom pupils imitated the articulations of the teacher at the level of sound and the level of the movement of the organs of the mouth; two, the voice was trained through music; and three, students were trained to speak through audition (*Idiocy: Its Diagnosis*, 360). In teaching articulation, Seguin followed the precepts of Pereire, the deaf educator and proponent of oralism over sign language, in which pupils felt the shape of the mouth as articulation occurred.[6] Development of the voice was thought to proceed from the "animal voice" to the human voice where the "cries [of the pupil] are voices after all, they are the only beginning upon which we may be able to found the teaching of the speech; altering the cry into a medium voice, supporting that voice on successive consonants, and so on, preparing the materials of true speech out of the animal voice" (ibid., 355).

In seeking this "human voice" (learning to speak), music and audition played a significant role for the hearing student, because they returned attention to sensation. Alongside tactile methods, controlled movement of the mouth and the voice were also learned by singing along with music in groups. Seguin believed that the "idiot" was a savant when it came to music. In fact, the "idiot" "has a rhythm like music" ("Origin," 34). Her cries were easily transformed; the speechless "idiot" went from being monosyllabic to having an intense sensibility to music. The student learned to appreciate musical rhythm, then was taught to perceive the sounds of language and to listen intensely (*Idiocy: Its Diagnosis*, 352). Through lessons, "music ceased to be a passive pleasure, and became the unpleasant, irresistible propulsor of the voice" (ibid., 362).

Assuming the student could hear, Seguin asked that teachers give "perspicuity and continuity to audition" (*Idiocy: Its Diagnosis*, 354). But the

Figure 3.1. By the 1890s, pupils formed an asylum orchestra. The New York State Archives, Public Domain.

"idiot," it was thought, did not hear language normally; rather, according to Seguin, it was necessary to direct teachers to be exceptionally expressive, use extra emphasis on certain words and syllables, accentuate the accent so that the words the "idiot" heard acted forcibly upon the mind (ibid., 358). Because of the unique way the "idiot" heard, according to Seguin, the teacher should adapt her articulation to each student. Teachers were asked not only that "every word be invested with a different physiognomy in each command" but also to present the verb prominently, deploy the imperative mood often, and allow syllables to flow as musical notes (ibid., 481). Speech was deployed as a heightened sensation so that intellectual processes could be mediated by and intersect with physiological ones (ibid.).

While Wilbur reported that some pupils entered the school without any speech whatsoever—of 207 pupils who entered in 1875, for example, eighty-five had never spoken a word (24th *Annual Report*, 102)—few (if any) were reported to have come with skill in the intellectual use of language. That he does not offer any indication that pupils entered with sufficient speech or language abilities, however, does not signify that those pupils

Figure 3.2. Pupils performing exercises in front of a stage, circa 1890s. The New York State Archives, Public Domain.

did not exist. Additionally, it appears that some deaf or hearing-impaired students did attend, though I found no statistical report of them, and the pedagogy for those who could and those who could not hear appears to have dovetailed. Either way, Wilbur made persuasive appeals for support to the legislature (in the annual reports) by emphasizing the "ordinary" functioning of pupils in his reports only as evidence of success. Thus, he categorized incoming pupils mostly as having neither effective use of speech nor the ability to use language as it related to reflection and intellect.

For those who could speak, recitation became an important method of enacting speech learning. Students often learned to recite the Lord's Prayer (6th *Annual Report*, 27). Speech was not the only indicator of success in the program. Case no. 12, A. M., made inarticulate sounds but grew quieter as his education proceeded. He was considered a success even without having learned to speak because he was more quiet and patient upon his return home (15th *Annual Report*, 49). Nattie and Willie, who were taken from Randall's Island having not yet acquired the capability to articulate words correctly, performed a pantomime show recounting a piece of Bible history (6th *Annual Report*, 26).

Alongside his categorizations of speech ability, Wilbur often said that regardless of speech ability many pupils had "no idea of language." The two categories, "speech" and "idea of language" were listed separately on the Descriptive Register of Pupils for 1875–79. "No idea of language" signified that the pupil perhaps could articulate sounds but could not comprehend, use, or integrate verbal cues into the reflective process. The "merely imitative" pupil was an example. Another example, Wilbur observed, was the pupil who could repeat entire words, sentences, and verses but had "no idea of the meaning of the words uttered, or even in some cases any idea of language proper" ("Relation," 35). Another pupil deployed "the speech of the parrot" or "echo speech" where they repeated the last words of sentences they heard or repeated sounds they heard prompted by their own or someone else's emotion.

If the pupil could move from this "mere" use of speech to understanding and using language alongside thought, they were thought to reach "a mode of ascendancy" that expanded opportunities to connect to others and to become "self-regulatory" (*Idiocy: Its Diagnosis*, 481). Language, not speech, was considered monumental, as it allowed one to achieve commonality with others; it was language, not speech, that allowed one to fully enter humanity ("Relation," 2). In treating language as civilizing and ascendant, Wilbur and Seguin followed a long line of classical and neoclassical thinkers such as Isocrates, Cicero, and Whately, who exalted language as a determinant of who could posses knowledge and who could possess civil authority (*Antidosis*, 75–79; *De Inventione*, I.II; *Elements*, 38). Cicero writes,

> To come . . . to the highest achievements of eloquence, what other power could have been strong enough either to gather scattered humanity into one place, or to lead it out of its brutish existence into the wilderness up to our present condition of civilization as men and as citizens, or, after the establishment of social communities to give shape to laws, tribunals, and civic rights? (*De Oratore* 33)

For Seguin and Wilbur, the uneducated "brute," and in this case the desecrated "idiot," needed to be civilized and this would happen when the pupil could use language—not simply speech—with skill and precision.[7] It is ironic, therefore, that speech teaching was foregrounded over language learning. By lessening the emphasis on the rhetorical uses of language, and focusing more heavily on the physiological mechanism of speech, the type of language education offered would obviously be quite limited. Speech was thought to be a necessity, but language lifted the beast even higher to join the rest of humanity. Wilbur and Seguin saw incoming pupils as needing to develop faculties required not just to become citizens, but to become—first of all—human.

Generally speaking, the pupils in the asylum-school were not asked to use language for the purpose of deliberation or for rhetorical purposes outside of day to day needs; speech acquisition was often considered sufficient if it gave the pupil some small measure of control over mundane decisions such as what clothes to wear and what food to eat. Wilbur reported on pupils' successes in the area of speech but not language use after they had received training in his program: one "deaf-mute" pupil "by the results of our training . . . now communicates with his companions by ordinary methods" ("Relation," 34). That is, the pupil spoke orally or "ordinarily" even though deaf. As previously mentioned, many students were said to have entered the school speaking, but only indistinctly. Thus, Wilbur attested with regard to their newfound learning that it allowed them to speak "quite distinctly." In the asylum-school, speech learning rather than use of language became the quintessence of education of the intellect; however, because Wilbur identified it as necessary to instill an idea of language into pupils, we know that he paid some attention to uses of language. Still, acquisition of speech was foregrounded in the curriculum over learning strategic and rhetorical uses of language, and this was the main limitation of rhetorical education for pupils at the asylum-school.

After Speech, Drawing, Writing, Then Reading

Following training in using the voice, in speech and minimal uses of language, the student was taught to draw. This would move the student toward both reading and writing. Within a broad notion of drawing, the student began by inscribing on surfaces as a sensorial technique. Drawing entailed more than simply wielding the pen or pencil; it included modifying surfaces, whittling wood, copying patterns, making marks, using the knife, chisel, hatchet, saw, and hammer. These inscription practices taught the representation of ideas as they were integrated *into* the substance in a tactile and sensory way, according to Seguin. Inscriptions of these types were expressive of meaning (*Idiocy: Its Diagnosis*, 386). The ideas of objects were represented by "carving, cutting, modeling, casting, and endless varieties of modes of expressing a meaning by lines on surfaces; those lines idealize matter" (ibid., 382). The lines that constituted drawing were soon transformed into the alphabet. The student learned the relative positions of circles, curvy lines, and straight lines while drawing in order to prepare to write. Real objects continued to guide the process, as "nature is his book, and his fingers are the printers" (ibid., 408). These experiential and sensorial processes were common also to nineteenth-century writing pedagogies in school-age children (Lucille Schultz, Elizabeth Mayo, John Frost) and in composition and rhetoric courses in college-level students (Albert Kitzhaber, Robert Connors).

After training in speech, drawing, and inscription, the student was then taught to write (which meant handwriting/orthography). Writing was taught before reading (Montessori and others followed this method of Seguin's), as writing was considered to be more visual and more connected to touch (the primary sensation) while reading was considered highly auditory and visual. Remember that Seguin generally taught through touch and sight before audition (for example, feeling the position of the lips and tongue in speech learning prior to listening to sounds); thus, writing was taught prior to reading. Imitation of the writing process was visual and tactile; the pedagogy relied upon the notion that memory is sensation. Also, students were taught to write only what they could say. In other words, the pupil had to first articulate verbally what he wished to write. The prior lessons in speech came to be useful here. The teaching of writing was also used to further speech. Seguin tells us that at Syracuse, "writing immobilizes *and* perpetuates both [speech and reading]" (*Idiocy: Its Diagnosis*, 405). Writing was used as another means to learn via the senses. What was said was written and thus seen by the eyes. What was seen by the eyes was then spoken. The whole word was learned in order to create precision with the sense of sight, and the letters and syllables were also learned as a sensorial exercise (ibid.). In these ways, writing became a verbal, visual, tactile, and also, ideally, an intellectual process. The teaching of writing was meant to be a practice that utilized less memory and more comparison, interaction, experience, and reflection (ibid., 397).

Alongside writing, reading was taught which returned to study of the voice and audition (*Idiocy: Its Diagnosis*, 76). Reading was learned with the use of concrete (three-dimensional) and printed alphabet boards; touch was encouraged. Each object from the concrete alphabet board was made to fit on the printed board. In this way, the teaching of writing and reading returned to Seguin and Wilbur's emphasis on the hand of the student. Use of the hand brought about "new ideas which daily die unshaped in their minds, for want of the power of realization by their hands" (ibid., 391). Through inscription and writing which led to reading, the pupil was meant to understand "the will of making." Ideas were thought to be produced within this sensorial process of seeing, feeling, hearing, moving, and acting. The sensorial process would, ideally, become one of knowledge making.

Parallels exist here with what the Roman educator Quintilian said about learning to read and write. Quintilian emphasized, as Seguin did, that young pupils needed to learn the shape of letters rather than memorize their location within words. Quintilian wrote, "It will be best for children therefore, to be taught the appearances and names of the letters at once, as they are taught those of men" (I.I.XXV–XXVI). He went on to advocate, like Seguin, that children hold and touch the letters as a way to inspire learning. The hand was guided by grooves, as if the pupil were inscribing in wax. Seguin described the necessity of real objects in making knowledge and in reading and writing: as Seguin observed at Syracuse, "Reading is taught first and last by words. The word written is read, the word pronounced is written; the speech flies like the thought, writing immobilizes and perpetuates both. . . . Therefore, ab initio [from the beginning], there has been no presentation of new objects, i.e. [no] discovery, without instant nomination; no nomination which was not simultaneous with discovery" (*Idiocy: Its Diagnosis*, 405, 415). Quintilian advocated something similar: "[The advanced student and/or the orator] will utter, as far as his subject will allow, nothing but what he has written or, as Demosthenes says, hewn into shape" (XII.IX.16).

Speaking, writing, and reading (learned in that order), Wilbur comments, should stimulate "simple intellectual operations, [where] their minds turn inwardly, and with the exercise of consciousness, become capable of comprehending the laws of mind. Their wills undergo a simultaneous development, through the reciprocating influences of intelligence and will" (1st *Annual Review*, 57). Yet this training of the intellect seemed to only go so far. Imitative ability, as an important and inclusive function, was put to use—perhaps too consistently—in learning to write. The pupil A. T. "displays considerable imitative faculty, in copying various figures from drawing cards upon the blackboard" (6th *Annual Review*, 21). From this grounding

Figure 3.3. Poster displayed at the 1901 World's Exhibition in Buffalo. The New York State Archives, Public Domain.

in imitation, training was then taken further, into penmanship and orthography which again utilized imitation. Many students, Wilbur reports, wrote with "a beautiful hand" or a "handsome hand." Figure 3.3 is an example of one pupil's attempt at orthography. The sample was pasted along with other student writing onto a cardboard poster and displayed at the Pan American World's Exhibition in 1901 in Buffalo.

While Seguin and Wilbur idealized writing and reading as modes of thinking and intellectualizing, the examples I have found of practices of student writing and reading point to more rote processes (chapter 4 will examine this in more depth). This occurrence of what today we might consider a default mechanism of falling back into familiar pedagogical practices rather than newly theorized ones is part of the larger history of instruction in common schools (Schultz) and in other specialized academies (Cobb; Gold) and universities (Johnson) during the nineteenth century. Schultz in particular goes into depth discussing the reasons that, while experiential and object-oriented pedagogy was present in the common schools, it was never fully taken up as time went on and also failed to manifest extensively in college curricula (79).

The same held for instruction in geography at the asylum-school, one of the last subjects attended to in the training of the intellect. Typical of instruction at most nineteenth-century schools, geography was taught through a type of imitation: pupils memorized "important points" on the map. Nattie and Willie, following their lessons, were subjected to a "severe and protracted examination in geography, embracing minute details in regard to the topography of most of the countries of the globe, and many particulars in regard to physical geography, and drawing maps upon the blackboard" (6th *Annual Review*, 26). Successes certainly were attained. But imitation was eventually meant to be set aside in speech training, drawing, writing, reading, and geography so that a "full" intellectual process—what was conceived of as "reflective"—could overtake any rote processes. In this ideal scenario, reflective processes would include decision making, deliberation, and negotiating. Seguin summarized in detail the way in which the intellect should be educated beyond imitation:

> Cries have been converted by music into voices; articulation was derived from personal imitation concentrated in the organs of speech by mimicry; speech was treated as a combination of voice and articulation enforced by wants; writing was deduced from objective imitation; reading was the result of the combination of both speech and writing; letters are taught only as a study of contrast and analogy between their shapes or between their sounds; reading begins by words, each word having a shape or configuration, a name, and a meaning: hence solidarity is established between writing, reading, speaking, and soon understanding; so that the learning of one of them carries with it the knowledge of all. . . . [T]o write and to read implies the understanding of that meaning; everything short of it is an imposition by the teacher, or an infirmity of the pupil. (*Idiocy: Its Diagnosis*, 406)

But there is little evidence that suggests that Seguin and Wilbur went to the point of theorizing or practicing education or training in the understanding of meaning on an intellectual level. That is, they fell short in their training of the intellect by failing to fully theorize how imitative practices were transformed into the rational processes of reflection, decision making, deliberation, and negotiation.

Regardless of any shortcomings, some of which I will discuss further in the conclusion to this chapter, study in the schoolroom within Seguin's pedagogical sequence of the 3 Rs readied pupils for the next step, which was moral training. In the procession from activity to intellect and finally to training of the will, moral edification accompanied entrance into the "common life," in which pupils ideally gained employment and took on other ordinary responsibilities of everyday life. This moral edification and fine-tuned persuasion of the will meant that the pupil could cross the threshold from isolation and what was conceived as a hollow existence into engagement in the active, useful, and ordinary life of everyday people.

The Excited Will of the Teacher, the Dull Will of the Pupil

3d. Infirm in afflictions and will

—"Origin and the Treatment and Training of Idiots"

Influencing the will was the culminating principle, the last in the sequence of Seguin and Wilbur's method of education. Use of the will, according to philosopher and rhetorician George Campbell, is a faculty useful for "passionate eviction, that vehemence of contention, which is admirably fitted for persuasion" (904). Seguin and Wilbur's prescribed use of the will works similarly as the vehicle for action; but it is the teacher who imposes the will onto a supplicant, at least at first.[8] When the teacher has successfully influenced the pupil's will, the pupil is ready for transition from the sensory and reflective into what Seguin called "the active life."

Seguin writes about the immoral will of the pupil prior to transformation: "That which most essentially constitutes 'idiocy,' is the absence of moral volition, superseded by a negative will; that in which the treatment of an 'idiot' essentially consists is, in changing his negative will into an affirmative one, his will of loneliness into a will of sociability and usefulness; such is the object of the moral training" ("Origin," 35). Seguin advocated transformation of the "reflex life," where one's life was in others' hands into the "self-regulating life" where one's own conscience ruled (*Idiocy: Its Diagnosis*, 234). The pupil's will was brought to self-regulation through the disciplined imposition of one person's will onto a weaker other. This imposition—persuasion—of the teacher's will onto the pupil is a dimension of any pedagogy; however, for the "idiot," influencing the will manifested in unique ways. Such influence, Seguin warned, was a form of "repression [that] cannot be avoided" (ibid., 466).

Obedience to the will of another was thought of as a voluntary action that eventually led to the lessening of authority (*Idiocy and Its Treatment*, 234). Similar to the way that the teacher who taught speech had a strong consciousness of how she herself used language, the will of the pupil was commanded by the teacher, as the pupil was "flashed by the look, made passionate by the voice, commented upon by the accent, strengthened by the articulation, imposed by the emphasis, and carried by the whole power of the stronger on the weaker will" (*Idiocy: Its Treatment*, 483). Proper moral functioning by the teacher was the key element, because her morality was willed upon the weaker other. Isocrates asserted this claim on behalf of the morality and virtue of the teacher in *Against the Sophists*. Isocrates also was a strong proponent of moral education in general.

The activity of the will was so important in the asylum-school education that it was said to undergird all other phenomena (9th *Annual Review*, 15). Wilbur wrote of the all-encompassing nature of the will, "Finally, one may witness in all cases a deficiency in the great exciting and regulating principle . . . the *human will*" (1st *Annual Review*, 53). His students, Wilbur argued, did not lack will: "The '*human will*' is very present as the foundation of and potential for human thought and action" (9th *Annual Review*, 15; Wilbur's italics). Rather, the pupil's will was thought to be weighed down by "torpor" and "disuse." Students were observed as entering the asylum-school in complete moral disarray. Wilbur observed of such lowliness that the mental life of the "idiot" "does not feel the motives of action that lie above the range of appetite or passion. It grovels, while it should rise in the scale of being. And while the spirit thus fails in a proper, active out-going, a crust of habits of inertia and indifference forms" (22nd *Annual Review*, 11). Even further, the "idiot" "has been so long borne down by degrading associations, whether in the family or in the public alms-house, that nothing short of superior accommodations furnished by those engaged in their elevation in the scale of being, will restore them to their legitimate position . . . as objects of pity and not of disgust" (3rd *Annual Review*, 96). Training of the will intended to raise the pupil up from so-called deplorable moral and social conditions.

Moving the Will: Order, Social Decorum, and Appearances

A popular philosophy called moral treatment was used as a remedy to activate the "idiots'" torpid volition and thus allow them, most of all, to become civically useful and to live a life of relation. For Seguin, "Moral education is nothing else than a revelation . . . the chef d'oeuvre of the art of human training" (*Idiocy: Its Diagnosis*, 469). In the asylum-school at Syracuse, moral treatment entailed schooling in social decorum, appearances, and in a limited aspect of "worldly" endeavors. Pupils performed the individual duties of hygiene, cleanliness, and etiquette. They were taught to be displeased at anything dirty, to be pleased with beauty, and to avoid gluttony (ibid., 330–31). The "idiot" was taught to taste her food slowly, sit erect at the small supper table, and smell the flowers in order not just to name them but also to enjoy their pleasant aromas. Moral training also entailed gaining a healthy, glowing countenance that reflected the "idiot's" intellectual and moral awakening (ibid., 294). His "intelligent countenance" should never be "hereafter defaced," Seguin wrote.

Pinel had described moral treatment as a certain kind of pedagogical coercion *without* "corporeal indignity" (*Idiocy: Its Diagnosis*, 294). Disorder was turned into order by engaging the attention, harmonizing the mind, and instilling a healthy sense of fear that was supposed to turn into rational regard (Pinel, 60, 108, 195). In addition to his focus on insanity, which was an umbrella term that at the time included "idiocy," Pinel advised minimizing the use of physical restraints. Likewise, William Tuke, whom Seguin only vaguely referred to in his writings, had emphasized benevolence as the preferred method over restraint and intimidation. In his article on moral treatment and benevolent theory, Louis Charland draws connections between Pinel and Tuke in the sense that both practiced moral treatment more within discourses of benevolence and spirituality than within medical discourse ("Benevolent Theory"). The methods used at Tuke's York Retreat, known as the birthplace of moral treatment, were an extension of a Quaker ethical code that had an austere and rigorous flavor (Charland, 65). Seguin's adherence to the doctrine of moral treatment evolved out of the work of Tuke and Pinel. Kindness and happiness were often the methods preferred over a demand for intellectual progress; as an observer from the Syracuse *Daily Courier* noted, at Syracuse "learning is made an entertainment, greater freedom, intimacy, and mutual kindness seems to exist more here than in any seminary of learning that we have ever visited" ("Visit of Board of Supervisors").

As such, moral treatment went beyond an education in speaking, music, writing, reading, and arithmetic: the social and moral aspects of Physiological Education, perhaps even more than language, were thought to give the "idiot" her humanity alongside everyone else. Moral treatment has a history that includes Philippe Pinel's work with the insane in Paris and William Tuke's work at the York Retreat in England (established 1796). In addition to Pinel and Tuke, Seguin pointed to the work of monks in Spain who cured mental disease by using moral treatment and nothing else: through the patients' "performance of simple and assiduous duties, an enlightened and sovereign volition" emerged (*Idiocy: Its Diagnosis*, 462). The moral treatment in Spain by monks, Seguin tells us, had been passed on in France by Pinel (ibid). Pinel was known almost mythically as the alienist (early psychiatrist) and educator who quite literally removed the shackles from insane patients at Bicêtre, the Paris Asylum for the Insane and Idiotic ("Idiocy as the Effect," 3). Pinel had published his *Treatise on Insanity* in 1801, which outlined moral treatment as the gradual transformation of a corrupted soul through a mild, kind, humane, and "regular system of discipline" that aimed to reorient a person's entire manner of life (*Treatise*, 108).

At the Syracuse asylum-school, pupils were neat and tidy in appearance, well fed, and taught all the manners and rules needed to live a seemingly respectful, common life. Training of the will was taken up in these ways in the dining room and the main hall in order to teach manners and acts of social decorum. After the morning school routine, pupils took a small lunch at eleven o'clock followed by a brief recess and more classroom activity. Dinner was then served at one o'clock and consumed a good chunk of time, since it was used as a time "to inculcate habits of decorum, of moderation, and general propriety" (2nd *Annual Review*, 106). School then resumed from three o'clock until half past four, when supper was served. Pupils were seated around small tables in order to mimic a family atmosphere. Seguin observed that at Syracuse, "being few at a family-like table, they have to wait long enough to give each one the chance of controlling the beast which is inside his stomach; not so long as to let it loose in disgraceful manifestations" (*Idiocy: Its Diagnosis*, 495). Visitors to the school could observe that practices in social decorum drew an "idiot" out of his base instinct and into a higher scale of being (8th *Annual Review*, 10). Pupils were lauded for their ability to be orderly, prompt, and decorous in the schoolroom and at the table in the dining room (2nd *Annual Review*, 53). Decorum was taught as a series of kairotic moments in which doing the "right" or "correct" thing was advocated; however, those kairotic moments were not conveyed in terms of language use (as previously discussed) but rather in terms of social grace and manners.

Pupils came to the asylum-school, according to Wilbur, lacking just these skills. He recounts a visit he made to retrieve a pupil:

> After seeing him at his home, in a cellar in New-York city, standing, with an effort at concealment, partly behind the door, devouring, rather than eating a piece of bread, with the saliva running out of his mouth, ill clothed, and not over clean, and with a nervous twitching about the face, I candidly told the gentleman who accompanied me, that I felt some reluctance at including him among the number of experimental pupils. Nevertheless, he was allowed to come, and I ought properly here to enter my acknowledgement, that I was entirely mistaken in his case. We have now no more promising pupil. . . . His whole appearance is changed. There has been a radical change in his habits of body and mind. He is very playful; very attentive in his various mental exercises, and conducts himself, under all circumstances, with propriety. (2nd *Annual Review*, 153–54)

A large portion of the pupils were unable to dress or undress themselves, and some were unable to feed themselves with propriety upon first entering the asylum (1st *Annual Review*, 45). In one instance, Wilbur traveled to Randall's Island Asylum to bring "Nattie" and "Willie" back with him. Wilbur wrote that he felt compelled to hurry "them into the bathing room, to be washed, and brushed, and combed, and aproned" (2nd *Annual Review*, 143). Wilbur delighted in declaring that, after training in his school, the two boys showed a "pleasing improvement in manners and deportment" (3rd *Annual Review*, 79).

Case No. 7 (1853) involved a boy who improved in the moral arena. Due to his propensity to steal, the boy necessitated a daily search through his pockets. Wilbur observed him as being quite inventive in his thievery. But, Wilbur tells us, through sustained moral treatment his moral character improved and his thieving ceased (2nd *Annual Review*, 136–38). Another pupil, C. E., "now associates with our best class of pupils" (6th *Annual Review*, 24). Moral training raised pupils up on the scale of being through rigorous training in social decorum and ethical action. And, after evening supper where these manners and ways of being were perfected, everyone returned to the main hall to engage in tasteful dancing, singing, games, music, and entertainment.

A Discourse of Rights and Participation in Worldly Affairs

Seguin located moral training alongside social decorum within a discourse of rights; he perceived an intrinsic worth of individuals, what he called "the unit man," and his trinitarian hypothesis attempted to develop the pupil in that liberal democratic image (*Idiocy: Its Diagnosis*, 172). Seguin referred to Benjamin Franklin and Thomas Paine as having influenced his work insofar as it embodied an expression of the rights and responsibilities of man in society (*Idiocy and Its Treatment*, 37). He meant that man had a responsibility to educate all people, but he also meant that all people had a responsibility to serve society. He wrote that we establish "the limits of his capacity, social relations, rapports sociaux, whose ever-changing scale is expressed by the two fixed words, rights and duties" (*Idiocy: Its Diagnosis*, 474). Sensory, mobility, and intellectual training civilizes and socializes, but moral training transports the "idiot" from isolated "mass" to a social being who has similar rights and responsibilities to the common "man." Seguin further framed moral training within a discourse of rights and responsibilities by comparing socialization and education of the "idiot" to that of "women, Jews, peasants, Sudras, Parias, Indians, Negroes . . . [who] are not now denied a soul, as they were once by religious or civil ordinances" (ibid., 444–45). It had been determined likewise that the "idiot" had a soul, a will, and thus, the ability to self-regulate his consciousness and actions. The "idiot" could possibly reside within the discourse of civil rights.

Moral treatment also taught that the pupil had to learn to manage a small bit of worldly affairs (*Idiocy: Its Diagnosis*, 155). Seguin explained, "We send them to make experimental purchases with their own earned money, and let them and the other children debate together the result of these foreign operations" (ibid., 499). This reference to "debate" is atypical, but does show one instance of how pupils engaged in reflection and deliberation. To further experience the world outside the asylum, Seguin advised that students should visit museums, churches, theatres, and parks in order to cultivate social knowledge and social graces (ibid., 266). They were expected to learn how to engage in small talk and to be polite, self-sufficient, decorous, cultured, worldly, and well-mannered. They learned to enjoy the sights and amusements of the city (3rd *Annual Report*, 94). The site of the asylum had been chosen so that the city was nearby, yet far enough away to allow for a safe, segregated environment. Of utter importance was that the asylum was located close enough to local places of worship that services could be attended by older, more advanced students (ibid., 32). The annual report of 1877 noted that boys were allowed small traveling expenses in order to go out into the world and perform tasks for the "household."

To fulfill certain rights and duties as a citizen, the pupil was taught to live the active life, including how to become useful, instruction that, Seguin believed, contained the potential to make men free. He enlisted pupils in fulfilling rights and duties by way of contributing to society. The proper education then created the opportunity for action so that acting in the world was all that could be done (*Idiocy: Its Diagnosis*, 74). For example, Seguin wrote, "we often send some children to carry objects of comfort to a destitute family in the neighborhood" (ibid., 502). He goes on to explain that "our serving [them] teaches them to serve others" (495).

Action was a human obligation; humanity, civility, and ethical action were achieved through learning to act in the world. And, action was always performed mutually and in relation to others. The "idiot," Seguin tells us, responded well to the law of mutual dependence ("Origin," 2). The asylum attempted to give pupils, particularly boys (consistently, two-thirds of the pupils at the asylum were male), an education, which was the "highest want of any individual in a Republican State" (2nd *Annual Report*, 67). Boys and girls both were not released from the rights and duties accorded to them by liberal humanism, for "they have a human soul, a human destiny" (1st *Annual Report*, 56).

The Farm and the Sewing Room

To further fulfill the role of the contributing citizen within a republican state, the pupil would be readied for useful occupation. Employment or occupation had a social element and a moral status to it (*Idiocy: Its Diagnosis*, 496); work was an important civic duty pupils had to fulfill, for if they escaped "the law of work," they could not be considered to have attained the status of the "unit man" (ibid., 498). After failing to educate him, Itard damned the Wild Boy of Aveyron to a life of uselessness: "Go expatriate your misfortune, die of misery and boredom at Bicêtre" (Itard, 73). But Seguin corrected Itard, arguing that if the pupil was not made useful, then it was the fault of the teacher ("Idiocy as the Effect," 4).

Work on the farm was a large part of moral treatment for boys. Many boys and men were considered civically useful because they could be productive laborers on the farm. For the first few years at Syracuse, the asylum maintained a farm through external paid labor consisting of one gardener and two farmhands. By 1857, hired farm labor was accompanied at work by pupils. In the first annual report, the board of trustees assert that "idiots may be so trained and instructed as to render them useful to themselves and fitted to learn some of the ordinary trades, or to engage in agriculture . . . and in all cases almost without exception, they can be made cleanly and neat in their personal habits, and enjoy many of the comforts of life, while they will cease to be regarded as encumbrances, and annoyances to the families in which they reside" (1st *Annual Report*, 12). In 1857, it was reported that the asylum farm would soon be fully productive due to the labor of pupils (14).

The farm supplied all of the asylum's vegetables. Boys of all ages worked the farm so that, like M. A. and L. S., they would "undoubtedly be capable in a few years of useful labor on a farm" and "will soon be in a condition to be bound out to a farm" (6th *Annual Report*, 22–24). By 1859, the farm's capacity was further increased with the boys' labor, which was considered to have "incidental economic results," of which the state approved (8th *Annual Report*, 8, 11). In 1860, the asylum leased thirty-five acres in order to expand the farm. Case no. 13, F. P., was released at age nineteen to work on a local farm (15th *Annual Report*). No trades had been formally introduced by 1857, although pupils had been performing industrial functions such as housework, farmwork, grading, and digging for most of the asylum's existence. By 1880, the farm supplied all the winter and summer needs of the asylum household (29th *Annual Report*, 40). In addition to farm labor, by 1880, boys worked in a newly established shoe shop and brush shop, where they more than repaid their living expenses (29th *Annual Report*, 41). By that time, industrial training constituted the majority of the curriculum. A year before Wilbur's death, the Fairmont Farm was purchased—the institution's first "colony," located four miles from the asylum itself. The "inmates" collected stones for the cellar walls after they had excavated the earth (32nd *Annual Report*). The older boys built a farmhouse there, where forty of them would live and work. This was common practice in the nineteenth century when it came to building or assisting in building and maintaining schools, although it has yet to be fully examined in our histories of rhetorical education.

By 1858, while the boys worked on the farm, the girls did most of the "family sewing" (7th *Annual Report*, 24). Wilbur considered them successful "producers." Wilbur assessed the girls' early productive capacities: "We have a class of girls in sewing for an hour each day. Some of the little girls can do little more than hold a needle in their hands or even a piece of cloth, but they gradually acquire a curiosity to notice what the others are doing, and will in the same gradual manner make the first attempts towards sewing. During the summer past, the elder members of the class have made twenty-four sheets; twenty-four towels; forty pillow-cases, besides hemming

Figure 3.4. Women ironing, circa 1890. The New York State Archives, Public Domain.

a large number of pocket handkerchiefs. Their success already gives promise that they will in time be able to do much of the sewing required in such an institution" (2nd *Annual Report,* 102). Sewing, it was thought, had the power to dissipate "wayward propensities" (ibid., 17–19). In 1866, forty feet were added to the rear of the main building, as was a new workroom for industrial occupations, and a new, large sewing room and an enlarged laundry. By 1880, the girls performed the necessary housework and sewing to accommodate the asylum (29th *Annual Report,* 42).

In the institution's annual reports and in his own writings, Wilbur reiterated over and over that this type of civic usefulness was *the* main goal of education at the school. Promoting usefulness not only benefited the pupil but also society as a whole, according to Wilbur and Seguin. Wilbur attested, "I desire only that they may have such an education as they are capable of, an education of the most practical character, promoting their usefulness, their happiness and the public good" (2nd *Annual Report,* 79).

Wilbur reported some successes in the area of civic usefulness: Case no. 15, S. G., orphaned, nursed her foster mother, who had become an invalid. After further training at the school, she certainly would be "through her life comparatively serviceable as a member of society" (29th *Annual Report*). Autonomy often measured how useful a pupil could be. Cases no. 23 and no. 24, two boys C. C. and G. W., arrived at the school together in 1859, made progress in the schoolroom and in outdoor work. Both left to support themselves working on the canal. They visited the asylum frequently until one died, which prompted the other to enlist as a soldier (15th *Annual Report*). Both boys lived what would have been considered a useful and valuable life. Case no. 25 arrived in 1856 and was employed full time on the farm, where "he rendered valuable service." After leaving the asylum, in 1863 bounty hunters kidnapped him and enlisted him in the army at City Point. Wilbur tells us that this case marked the fourth pupil who had served in the army since the start of the war (15th *Annual Report,* 59). Army service proved that moral treatment at the asylum had been successful. The common life was, indeed, possible for some, however voluntary or involuntary an activity such as conscription may have been.

On the farm, in the laundry room, and in the sewing room, Wilbur intended to give pupils "useful employment" and also provisional integration into the city proper. Social and moral obligations were met through work on the farm and in the sewing room, and more generally, in the achievement of a capacity for usefulness. Persuasion of the will through moral treatment ensured that pupils became useful, pleasantly decorous, and well mannered, so that they could serve the asylum, their families, the city, and the nation. Moral treatment and training of the will moved pupils' range of activity and relations farther outward to include a more complex and intereconnected life of relation. In the early years of the asylum-school, many pupils graduated and returned to live with their families in the communities from where they had come.

Burgeoning of the Asylum

But even as many pupils were leaving the asylum after "successful" treatment and entering the "common life" or "the active life," as early as 1860 Wilbur's reports betrayed a trace of despondency on his part, as he forsaw the abandonment of a large portion of the educational ideals I have discussed in this chapter. In his report to the legislature in 1860, he lamented, "Another year has passed in the history of the asylum" (8). As superintendent, as guardian, of such "unfortunate" yet promising souls, Wilbur already had to contemplate the imminent growth of asylums, including his own, which would nearly obliterate the system of progressive education and replace it with industrial training that maintained the institution as a custodial warehouse for low-level labor, or worse, as an abyss nearly entirely severed from society. Early on, Wilbur was against custodialism, uncurtailed growth, and decentralizing of the schoolroom: in 1852, he pleaded that "our asylum is not to be regarded in such a light" as to be purely vocational; instead, he asserted early in the institution's history that the asylum was an educational facility, a school, not a hospital or asylum for incurables (1st *Annual Report*, 42).

In order to maintain an intimate, family-like educational setting that he could justify by reporting successes, in the early years of the school, Wilbur admitted only those he thought could learn or be rehabilitated. In the early years, in fact, he did not believe that any of his chosen pupils were incurable or unteachable. By 1857, he was still "not yet ready to admit the existence of exceptional cases which may be called incurable" (6th *Annual Report*, 66). Throughout the early years of his institution, he repeatedly told the legislature that "all the pupils have improved" (2nd *Annual Report*, 9). But in 1857 one pupil was removed because of what was deemed an incurable nature (12). The "lower grade idiot" could not achieve the goals of educating the activity, intellect, and the will. This realization of incurability, along with the steadily increasing number of pupils that were admitted, began to alter the priorities of the school, to Wilbur's evident chagrin.

By 1872, Wilbur admitted that a few more cases were in fact "incurables" and that those who were less educable should be placed in a custodial institution—not at his school (21st *Annual Report*, 43–45; 56–58). Besides acknowledging that there were pupils in his school that would only tangentially benefit from his course of study, Wilbur also acquiesced to enlarging the school and accepting the board of trustees' push to subordinate school exercises to the upkeep of the "more practical objects of the institutions" (11th *Annual Report*, 13).

To contextualize Wilbur's struggles with custodialization and growth, Wolf Wolfensberger, in *The Origin and Nature of Our Institutional Models*, demarcates three periods of asylum growth. First, there was the educational period which ran approximately from 1848 to 1870. The pity period followed, lasting roughly from 1870 to 1890, with the social menace period assuming domination close to 1884, although it had certainly begun, with subterfuge, quite earlier (28–39). Wilbur was caught in a tide of custodialization and change, in the face of which he could maintain little control. His discourse, and his decisions, reflected the changes that Wolfensberger postulates. In 1872, Wilbur used the term *inmates*—apparently, for the first time—to describe the "hospital cases" (21st *Annual Review*, 59).

While Wilbur tried to place limits on the number of pupils that the school would admit, he simultaneously took part in planning for additional buildings and expansion of space. In his *Report to Enlarge the Asylum* in 1866, he mentioned the forty feet added to the rear of the main building, the large schoolroom added onto the main story (rather than a small, intimate schoolroom, which had been the norm), new hospital accommodations on the second story, and two large dormitory rooms above the hospital (14). In 1877, additional structures included a brand new building on the north side to accommodate all "large" boys, a workroom for industrial occupations, a large sewing room, an enlarged laundry, and residences for laundresses (27th *Annual Report*). These new accommodations, he noted, "allowed us to give greater prominence to industrial occupations both for girls and boys" (28th *Annual Report*).

In 1852, Wilbur's school in Albany had forty-six pupils. In the first annual report, it was apparent that, though the board of trustees were in favor of expansion, he himself did not necessarily want a larger building that might accommodate more pupils (15). Four years later, Wilbur stated that a school such as his should never admit more than one hundred pupils (5th *Annual Report*, 63). Despite this and declarations like it, the number of pupils increased as follows: 1852: 46 pupils; 1862: 130; 1872: 153; 1879: 274; 1883: 316; 1930: 1,437 (this statistic from 1930 is less relevant for this discussion, but shocking nonetheless). The asylum's numbers increased over the latter years due to the growth of the eugenics movement, which created an air of fear around embodied differences.[9] Much of this was beyond Wilbur's control. The eugenics movement supported social and educational policy that "scientifically" determined who was fit for society and who was not. The numbers sent to asylums increased as more people were deemed statistically unfit under the "science" of Henry Goddard's intelligence quotient test, which gained prominence around the turn of the twentieth century.

However, in the earliest years of the school, even before the fear tactics of the eugenicists took a deep hold, the number of students continually increased in response to Wilbur's professed successes, even though he had stated that the school should never house more than one hundred pupils (5th *Annual Report*, 63). It appeared that as Wilbur proclaimed more and more that incurables and unteachables were in fact a "reality," the industrial nature would exceed the educational one. In Albany among the board of trustees, some of whom were legislators, political will favored the expansion of Wilbur's school in order to increase revenue from farm production, sewing, the shoe repair and brush and caning shops, and other domestic production. Finally, in 1880, due to an increased population, it was recorded that for the first time "[t]he farm and garden have in the main supplied the wants of the household not only in the way of summer vegetables but also for the winter use" (29th *Annual Report*, 40). As the industrial curriculum grew, more pupils could be admitted without hiring more paid employees, because the pupils now were doing nearly all the work to maintain the asylum. Additionally, in 1880, Syracuse opened a satellite asylum for girls that functioned as the custodial facility, and the State Board of Charities[10] forced Syracuse to conform to its standards, following which Wilbur's voice in the annual reports appears to have become less and less influential.

By 1880, rather than claiming successes as he had before, Wilbur reported only "tolerable success." Perhaps due to his acknowledgment of the existence of unteachables, he began to express doubts about his previous educational successes and thus acquiesced to the board of trustees' push for an emphasis on industrial instruction at the expense of common school and liberal arts instruction (29th *Annual Report*, 57). His doubts may be more clearly understood in the context of a resurgence in belief in the existence of "unteachables," especially by the board of trustees, who wrote that "the presence of these not only embarrasses the general management, but swells the average cost of taking care of the pupils" (18th *Annual Report*, 11). Further, it was said that "disappointments have arose from the amount of unteachables, more than originally thought" (19th *Annual Report*, 11).

In 1883, his last year as superintendent, which was also the year of Wilbur's death, the report by the board of trustees rationalized modifications to the original purpose and scope of asylum:

> There seems to be some misapprehension in the public mind upon this subject. . . . The casual visitor to an asylum may go away with the impression that the mental exercises are predominant. The term "school" sometimes applied to such institutions may have fostered the idea. However if an inquiry is made by such visitor, he will be told, at once, that such exercises are only means to an ultimate

> end; and that, to make the pupils capable of some employment. He will be told that mental training is subordinated and contributory to that main purpose. Even the amusements are made to subserve the same ends. . . . So predominating is the practical training in our institution that if the term "school" were applied at all, it should be industrial school for idiots. (32nd *Annual Report*, 4–6)

After Wilbur's death in 1883, the social menace model replaced his original educational modus operandi. The new superintendent, G. A. Doren, reported to the legislature from a deftly eugenic standpoint that expressed the desire to segregate "undesirables" so that they would not negatively influence the rest of society. Doren's philosophy deviated from that of Wilbur and Seguin in that Doren saw little potential for education in the population other than for the purposes of industry. Even further, Doren's eugenics-based policy sought to eradicate "idiocy" and feeblemindedness from humanity; he spoke overtly about his desire to end procreation among those deemed "idiotic." Doren wrote,

> [I]t will therefore be in no spirit of change, but rather in furtherance of [Wilbur's] plans that a co-ordination and extending of the benefits of this institution . . . that recommendation for increased accommodations and facilities are made. . . . No matter how much the individual may be elevated or improved, however, we do not feel nor believe that they should ever be encouraged to assume the social relations of life as the mentally strong. . . . They should be gently isolated and insulated . . . seeing to it, however, that their infirmities pass away with them. (33rd *Annual Report*, 13–15)

Doren expressed a mainstream belief of that time, which was in opposition to most of Wilbur and Seguin's work: that the "idiot" had little if any potential to achieve any other than vocational usefulness. Thus, custodialization and industrial training made more sense than an education in activity, intellect, and the will. This belief ultimately led to the abandonment of many of Wilbur and Seguin's ideals as I have discussed them in this chapter.

It was Seguin's methodical and well-recorded "physiological method" that Wilbur carried out with at least partial success at the school—particularly in the first few years, although less so as the years progressed. In the beginning, Wilbur had been particular in his method of educating the activity, intellect, and the will:

> We educate the senses till they perform their office with correctness, precision and celerity; we increase the faculty of imitation;

> we awaken the perceptions, seeking correct notions of surrounding and familiar objects; we excite a healthy curiosity; we cultivate the memory and comparison; we arouse the will by appropriate stimuli, producing activity, spontaneousness and self-reliance; we nourish the feeble flame of emotions, desires, affections, and a proper sense of right. During all this course, our ceaseless effort will be to reform improper habits and teach the proprieties of life. (1st *Annual Report*, 57)

Seguin and Wilbur saw pupils as having potentiality, their sensations alive and "calling forth for entrance." The schoolrooms were central to learning, and during the first ten to twenty years, they were small. But the time that followed Wilbur's death would enact entirely different methods, methods that would come to be deplored and resisted by the late 1940s. The ideals of Seguin and Wilbur, much further improved upon, would not rise again on a wide scale until the progressive education movement in the late 1960s and passage of the Individuals with Disabilities Education Act of 1975 (formerly the Education for All Handicapped Children Act). Seguin and Wilbur were in no sense flawless in their pedagogies, but they were certainly progressive for their time.

A Pedagogy of Sensation, Functional Action, and Participation

The complex model of "special" education I have just described embodies a systematic and institutionalized attempt to transform a person's physiological, psychological, intellectual, and moral nature into "something else." The body and its sensations lie at the core. Historically, education has consisted of the development of not only a second nature but also other generalizable imperatives: social relations, skill in everyday duties, interconnectedness with others, physical transformation, civic usefulness, effective use of language, control of the will, proper deportment, countenance, and decorum. While the education at the asylum-school performed many of these functions, it performed them in ways that not only help us earmark the origins of "special" education but also allow us to understand how "special" education has come to influence education in a broad sense.

First, by looking to the curriculum of the asylum-school, education can be seen as constituted by various acts that involve the acquisition of knowledge, regardless of its type or level. Education at the asylum-school helps us appreciate that no increment of knowledge, and no physical action is too minute, too basic, too sensorial, too functional, or too experiential or object-oriented to be considered as part of the learning curve. Learning is corporeal and material regardless of whether the body is moving in ways normatively prescribed. Sensation was indeed the starting point: first touch, then the other senses, then sitting, standing, walking, using the hand, then drawing, writing, and finally reading. Students were taught to write only what they could say; articulation was foregrounded. Feeling objects in the hand was meaningful; walking in the garden conjured ideas. Speech was paired with feeling the mouth move. Nuts and grapes were the *things* of mathematics.

The education inside the asylum-school taught one to act at the most micro or foundational level and the most sensorial and material level necessary or possible. It addressed the mind's and body's faculties at all stages and across a wide continuum. It considered basic physical movement, feeling, touching, seeing, hearing, and other foundational, though seemingly rudimentary, practices. This emphasis on a broad range of action and knowledge acquisition (physical and mental) allowed pupils to maneuver at a nonstandardized pace through the educational course; teachers adjusted the curriculum based on pupils' varied capacities and needs (2nd *Annual Report*, 53). The teacher's toolbox was greatly expanded, and intellectual and civic capacities were developed methodically, step by step along a broad spectrum of experience.

Second, this attention to bodily micro-actions allowed functional skills to maintain import. Corbett, in his study of John Locke's contributions to rhetorical theory, asks, "If the human mind does not come equipped with ideas, how does it acquire knowledge?" (Corbett, 425). Seguin and Wilbur contended that knowledge was first acquired through functional actions, which began in bodily sensation and movement. In their pedagogy, learning was always paired with physical action that had real-world purpose. One sniffed the flower in order to enjoy its smell. One learned that the marble was round so that it could roll on the table. In the asylum-school, this functional learning was never abandoned at any level of the intellectual process; rather, functional action formed the foundation for *all* acts and all knowledge making. We are reminded here that a reconsideration of the purposefulness of acts often leads to increased motivation and investment in their outcome.

Third, while speech and language were certainly taught at the asylum-school, a pupil's progress in those areas did not necessarily indicate whether or not they succeeded in the program. Verbal language was considered as that which facilitated entry into humanity and into public endeavors, yet in the school's curriculum, the absence of ordinary language abilities did not preclude participation and usefulness in public endeavors. This decentralizing of verbal language supports notions of multiple intelligences, by which we comprehend and value alternative and "unordinary" ways of communicating or being, leading to, for example, the idea that speaking and writing may not always be the only or the best means of achieving learning and understanding.

These concepts—a broad range of knowledge acquisition, the importance of functional action, and the decentering of language—and their application created a paradoxical type of education in the asylum-school. The education, certainly, centered around the *art of becoming*. However, rhetoric at this conceptual site cannot be conceived as verbal eloquence or as that which grants robust civic authority or civic equality. This was a baseline problem in the asylum-school—functional skills were not paired sufficiently with critical reflection. *Things* and *sensations* were emphasized over *ideas* to the point that ideas were nearly abandoned. Wilbur and Seguin found themselves instructing pupils in reflective action as it concerned muscles and coordination rather than reflective action that worked toward critical analysis of or critical engagement in one's surroundings. Wilbur and Seguin's rhetorical education was limited in numerous ways; however, it also provoked action that was progressive for that historical moment. It followed in the footsteps of the classical rhetoricians whose aims were most emphatically to cultivate civic participation, and it also addressed many commonplaces of nineteenth-century pedagogies.[11] Pupils who previously had been denied access to civic spaces and civic actions could now enter those spaces and now perform those actions.

The idea that only certain types of people could be civically active has been common throughout history. An example of this line of thought that has particular resonance with education at the asylum-school can be seen in George Campbell's assertion in the *Philosophy of Rhetoric* that "idiots and changelings" entirely lack access to common sense. Campbell wrote, "I own, indeed, that in different persons [common sense] prevails in different degrees of strength; but no human creature hath been found originally and totally destitute of it, who is not accounted a monster in his kind; for such, doubtless, are all idiots and changelings" (I.V.III). Clearly, Seguin and Wilbur disagreed. Campbell, writing in the century prior to Wilbur and Seguin's declaration that "idiots can learn," was working within a notion of common sense as part of the Stoic ethic that holds that individuals can achieve social harmony through participation in public life. Because educators in the mid-nineteenth century were working to fulfill promises of universal education, it became more possible for "idiots" to be understood as having access to the *sensus communis*. That is, the moral, intellectual, and social training at the school—training of the activity, intellect, and will—attempted to instill a sense of relation and interconnectedness between the previously isolated individual and the communities through which that individual could, but typically did not, circulate.

The asylum-school did, then, at least partially prepare students to be citizens, to participate in "civil society." But the education at the asylum-school only went so far. The purpose of the education was, to quote

Wilbur, "*not* to fill all the faculties that are wanting. Not to give an entire 'normal' social or moral life" (1st *Annual Report*, 15; my italics). Wilbur never envisioned his pupils as "capable of sustaining, creditably, *all* the relations of a social and moral life" (ibid., 55; my italics), but rather he wished only to have them attain some level of usefulness. As a comparative example, David Gold points to the ways that education at Texas Women's University (1901–1939) "greatly expanded [the students'] life options" (*Rhetoric at the Margins*, 278). The graduates at the university became teachers, wives, physicians, chemists, public citizens etc. (266). The graduates of the asylum-school were much more limited in their public roles: they became soldiers, cooks, farmhands, laundresses, housekeepers. They were not legally allowed to marry and were persuaded to not procreate. They participated in public life but only as helpers, laborers, assistants, "hands," and laymen. They were not able to move up in the ranks of the military, or for that matter, in any organizational structure.

This study helps us conceive of education in new ways, such that we are more attuned to varied pedagogies and how they are deployed in alternative educational settings, such as a nineteenth-century asylum-school, and within or on alternative corporealities such as the pupils at the school. While the curriculum overlapped with aspects of general education on many levels, an ongoing tension existed between more traditional conceptions of pedagogy and what I have shown were the dimensions of the curriculum at the asylum-school. That is, the pupils were not taught how to orate, write on a persuasive level, speak in public places, and were not even minimally taught to influence the political sphere. They knew how to judge and deliberate, but only in terms of the relation of objects to each other. They were not taught to critique, or for that matter, even to become conscious of the social arrangements that kept them disenfranchised economically and politically. They were not explicitly taught political theory or rhetorical theory or, as far as I can tell, how language was used rhetorically and ideologically; they were not taught to be citizen-orators, teachers, leaders, or organizers—at least in the normative ways we conceive of these roles. Because the pedagogy was limited in terms of the types of language use that were taught, pupils were considered also to lack the conceptualizing power needed to perform rational, deliberative civic acts.

Aristotle refers to phusiopoesis as potentiality (*On Rhetoric* 1.11). Isocrates reminds us that rhetorical wisdom evolved out of the acknowledgment that "power lies in the realms of the impossible" (72). But if education is enveloped in the urge to improve and in the realms of the impossible, is it sufficient to offer an education such as that at the asylum-school (or any education for that matter) that could be viewed as having significant limits?

As has often been the case historically for people with disabilities (as well as people without disabilities), educational methods exacted a price. As Brenda Brueggemann, Douglas Baynton, and multiple other scholars have pointed out, educational, rehabilitative, and rhetorical training are often achieved at the expense, more than to the benefit, of people who do not fit within normative modes of communication or bodily expression; the asylum-school curriculum dispensed an unintended violence to body and mind. That is, despite Wilbur's progressive benevolence and his supposed successes, the asylum-school must be viewed within the context of an education and language training marked by limitations, even denials, silences, and curricular injustice (more on this in the following chapter).

The asylum-school training was indeed a type of education where those deemed "abnormal" were set apart from the rest of society and asked to become entirely different, and supposedly better, people. Inside the asylum-school, rhetorical education became a highly manicured and monitored *willingness* and a Foucaldian sense of disciplining—a way of being in the world that entailed strict submission to a pedagogy from above. It entailed navigating a gauntlet of conform-at-all-costs and transform-or-go-home. However, while vocational participation was foregrounded in the asylum-school over participation in public deliberation or rhetorical uses of language, success was not entirely defined by language ability and pupils *were* able to expand their life options, regardless of how limited those options may have been. Study of the asylum-school's curriculum as rhetorical education demonstrates that we can—we must—expand our notions of who can be civically active and how this action manifests. Otherwise, we risk too-narrow definitions of engagement and we ignore salient educational methods that include sense impressions, the body, functional action, and a "special" appreciation of participating in the world.

CHAPTER 4

In Pursuit of the Underlife of an Archive

I was lonesome here all the time.

—E. S. (Letter 30, 1866)

Introduction

Thus far I have shown how rhetoric shaped commonplace arguments regarding the institutionalization of people in asylums in the mid-nineteenth century. I have considered the Syracuse asylum-school's curriculum as ideologically focused on sensations, experience, functionality, and the body. While discussions of commonplace arguments and curricular intentions are important, they nevertheless form an incomplete picture: while the majority of the surviving written evidence recounts the perspective of the institution and its philosophical founders, I cannot exclude the testimonies of the asylum school's pupils and their families, even though they are difficult to locate. This chapter attempts, then, to recover perspectives from "below," or those seemingly lost among the medicalized discourses of the histories of asylums. That these perspectives are not easily accessible spurs the questions: How do we complicate a one-sided historical record? How do we give presence to participation that has no written record? How do we historicize what seems to be silent and absent? This chapter "listens"[1] to that which is seemingly silent by filling in the gaps within bureaucratic rhetoric to give voice to families and pupils.

In the chapter I look at bureaucratic letter writing, because it is the only letter-writing evidence left in the historical record; but my intention is to also look *beyond* these bureaucratic inscriptions. I am guided by the questions: What has become of the five thousand pupils who lived at the asylum and their families? How does the written as well as the silent rhetoric I mine in the letters help us determine how rhetoric creates and is created by, and reinforces and resists, dynamics of power and social affiliation? I look at thirty-four letters, in three groups. The first group consists of twenty-three letters written by Superintendent Wilbur, the asylum's matron, its steward, and a few teachers to Mrs. Mary Thornton of Cincinnatus (and later Caton), New York, between 1855 and 1866 regarding her institutionalized son, Jimmy Thornton. The second group consists of ten letters written by family members and "friends" to the asylum's administration and teachers between 1853 and 1867. The third group consists of two texts (one letter) written by asylum pupils and displayed at the Pan American Exhibition in Buffalo in 1901.[2]

All of the letters comprise a kind of bureaucratic rhetoric (rhetoric that has gone through the filter of the institution), even though some of them were written by families and pupils. This is not to say, however, that the sentiments expressed in the letters written by the institution do not demonstrate sincerity and benevolence with regard to how much Wilbur and the asylum staff were invested in and cared about their pupils. Language that in one sense is sincere and in the other sense mechanistic and artificial is the paradox of rhetoric itself.[3] Put differently, rhetoric is a complicated amalgam of competing forces and actions (both discursive and material) that can be contradictory—another example being that rhetoric can simultaneously reflect both "reality" and appearance. Just as the education I have detailed in chapter 3 is neither wholly liberating nor wholly oppressive, rhetoric more generally is similarly complex and seemingly incongruous. In *Rhetoric at the Margins*, David Gold alerts us to the fact that rhetoric is not just hegemonic but also, simultaneously, subversive (8). Susan Kates's definition of "activist rhetorics" exemplifies this intricacy of the kind of rhetoric that is governed by oppositional forces. Kates defines activist rhetorics as "rhetorical study that pursues relationship between language and identity, makes civic issues a theme in the rhetoric classroom, and emphasizes the responsibility of community service as part of the writing and speaking curriculum" (xi). This definition taxonomizes one type of rhetoric (i.e., activist rhetorics) that works *against* hegemonic power.

However, a rhetoric of participation in the context of this collection of thirty-four letters involves a seemingly fraught communicative enterprise. Rhetoric is the negotiation that we engage in with each other, privately and civically and individually and collectively, to attempt to reconcile our multiplicitous understandings of "truth" and "reality." Rhetoric is silence as much as it is articulation, and I demonstrate how a deepening of our understanding of rhetoric can open the path to retrieve the subaltern "voices" of families and pupils of the asylum-school. Rather than defining rhetoric as simple jargon or verbal persuasion, a revised understanding values rhetorical inquiry as a complex and multilayered epistemological and methodological tool for negotiating gaps and silence in historical evidence in order to acknowledge various versions of "reality." Rhetorics, then, include language practices, bodily performances, and symbol usages that operate within systems of power, but they *also* entail barely audible traces, invisible performances, and non-extant experience that leave no tangible evidence. Rhetoric encompasses multiplicitous *uses* of language (utterance or enunciation) but rhetoric is also the existence of silence, which—and this is crucial—must not necessarily be confused with absence.[4]

John Duffy confirms this understanding of rhetoric as a sort of contest (a fight to be heard) in which meaning and identity are central to the dispute. He writes that rhetorics are "the ways of using language and other symbols by institutions, groups, or individuals for the purpose of shaping conceptions of reality . . . rhetorics are the languages of ideologies and offer symbolic means through which ideologies become known and are imposed, shared, understood, and overthrown" (*Writing from These Roots*,15, 17). Duffy's expansive definition, as well as the other notions of how rhetoric works (Gold, Kates, Berlin, Glenn), points to our need to acknowledge which "conceptions of reality" families and pupils/inmates of institutions experienced and how those "realities" may have differed from the dominant rhetorics of the institution. I am moved also to understand how these competing rhetorics are themselves multiplicitous. My understanding of rhetoric functions throughout this chapter, and more largely throughout this book, as complexities of discursive and material actions that never mean just one thing but rather are constituted by a push and pull of power that is enmeshed in complex social relations.

At first glance, when examining only what has been written in these letters, the pupils and their families appear somewhat silent and acquiescent. My point in this chapter is to show that while families and pupils may be silent in the historical record, in no way were they absent or entirely acquiescent.[5] Within the historical record of the asylum-school, although the dominant group is by and large the only voice that survives, that is not to say that the subordinate group (families and pupils) never spoke, wrote, or engaged in rhetoric. Because silence is imposed on people in the historical record, we can assume that, as Cheryl Glenn suggests in *Unspoken*, silence might be an expression of a multitude of things: agreement, disagreement, lack of information, lack of power, anger, doubt, empathy, and more (16).

I explore silence as generating endless ontological possibilities for creating presence in the face of what seems to be absence. In bringing silence to light, Jacqueline Jones Royster writes in *Traces of a Stream* that for her, "[t]he immediate challenge is to make visible many features, factors, relationships, people, and practices, that heretofore were not visible—to articulate what is there and what seems to be going on . . . to make better sense" (8). Meaning is made and gaps are filled through generating a sense of the fact of "being" whether or not we know the particulars of the story or the particulars of the lives and histories we are trying to recover.

Layers of Discourse

Vicki Collins's notion of "rhetorical accretion" is instrumental here, because while the letters were written by staff and administration, I look beyond the layers of institutional discourse they contain to uncover the perspectives of the families and pupils. Rhetorical accretion, according to Collins, is that which asks us to sort through the layers of rhetoric that mediate language farther away from its source. In "The Speaker Respoken," Collins conceives of rhetorical accretion as a feminist method that comes into play when

> the production authority sometimes decides to combine [voices]—for example, to attach an introduction representing a certain ideological viewpoint, to include a dedication indicating who supported the writer, or to publish a work in a volume with other works rather than as a solo text. This process of layering additional texts over and around the original text I call rhetorical accretion. . . . As in the accreted growth of stones by the addition of external particles, rhetorical accretion attempts to form a whole from disjointed parts. But unlike the natural process of mineral formation, textual accretion is the result of human agency. With each accretion to a text, the speaker of the core text is respoken. Respeaking can be a way for the production authority to modify the ethos of the original speaker or call into question something in her text. (548)

While Collins refers to texts that have been physically altered by someone other than the author, I extend rhetorical accretion to signify that I am able to access—and thus to make meaning from—the words or sentiments of pupils and their families only through the textual lens of the institution. Without direct access to words or sentiments of the pupils themselves or their families, I am forced to derive information from gaps and from second- and third-person accounts rather than from primary perspectives.

Because I can never truly know the exact words of the pupils and families, I infer multiple (sometimes contradictory) possible realities in terms of what they might or might not have written, said, or experienced. This work requires claim making akin to imaginative reconstruction or dramatic reconstruction, wherein I look for traces and make inferences and probable claims based on those traces.[6] The method recognizes, in the traditions of Frederich Nietzsche, Hayden White, Jacques Derrida, and Michel de Certeau, the rhetorical and narrative nature of all history writing in the sense that what we think of as history is always incomplete, emplotted, and inclined toward particular, that is to say, dominant, standpoints.

Overview of the Letters

The thirty-four letters that I examine have much layering to sort through; they are part of the institution's public face—they all have been selected, edited, and then published for public consumption in annual reports and professional settings and therefore, not surprisingly, construct the institution's ideology as concordant and harmonious with everyone who is involved in its functioning. Quite possibly, the letters survived and appear in the archive because of their agreeable nature and the fact that, at least on the surface, they depict harmonious relations between families and the asylum. Or perhaps *The James Thornton Correspondence* survived a fire[7] that other letters did not survive, or possibly a staff member had a particular fondness for Jimmy Thornton—our main character in this chapter—that compelled him or her to salvage the letters, or maybe a distant family member came to claim the letters, or perhaps an antique collector stumbled upon them at a sale.[8]

Those letters in this chapter that were written by families are best framed as petitions: they are appeals directed toward a higher authority (the asylum), and they request a particular action. Families wrote not only to gain admittance for their child, but once the child had been admitted, they wrote in order to obtain information as to the child's well-being, maintain some connection amid physical absence, acquire permission to visit, and request release. In addition to the letters of petition, a small sampling of the family letters are letters of gratitude. The letters written by the asylum staff and administration can be framed initially as educational progress reports written as responses to family petitions for information. The asylum responses, however, while couched in the genre of educational progress reports, functioned more as a means to gain acquiescence and consent from the family and to give advice, regulate visits, and maintain command to ensure continued institutionalization of the pupil. The letters worked to uphold and legitimize the life of the institution. As Phil Ferguson notes in "The Doubting Dance" with general regard to letters from asylums to families, institutions would typically try to be as nonoffensive or non-off-putting to the family as possible (4). This was the best way to gain consent and maintain leverage in the face of what most likely was recurrent resistance to and displeasure with institutionalization.

Because of the complex relationship between the asylum and the families, which certainly included accord as well as discord, each letter exhibits conventions that are unique to these three genres (petitions, letters of gratitude, and educational progress reports) and also unique to the environment and habits of asylums. In essence, however, all of the letters regardless of genre and particular habits embody the rhetoric of a less powerful entity (the family) appealing to an assumed authority (the asylum). The rhetoric between sender and receiver reproduces the hierarchical cultural system of institutions, in which the superintendent is a renowned physician who is reputed to know what is best for the child, and the family approaches him and his colleagues with a rhetoric of deference, graciousness, and humility.

A hierarchical relationship in letters is a common theme in scholarship. Carol Poster's and Carol Lipson's work on epistolary rhetoric is useful here, as is Suzanne Spring's work on letter writing at Mount Holyoke Female Seminary from 1837–1861.[9] Poster discusses how epistolary writing is more often theorized in terms of the social affiliations of the letter writers than in terms of the arguments made by them (3). And Lipson concurs in her discussion of ancient Egyptian rhetoric when she offers the compelling theory that Egyptian letter writers "enact a cultural understanding of the hierarchical roles and obligations of societal members" (87). Both argue that epistolary rhetoric has historically been focused on how letter writers navigate social hierarchies. Lipson goes on to explain that "this mundane genre" of bureaucratic letters (mundane because of the repetitive formalism she refers to in Egyptian letters) demonstrates a "rhetoric of accommodation," which assuages social and cultural conflict and nurtures concord at all costs (92). Spring's work, which examines the "culture of letters" at Mount Holyoke, demonstrates something quite different: women cultivated relational and reciprocal social relationships through writing likely because of their sense of equality among each other. In the asylum letters, the rhetoric, while benevolent and courteous, is less reciprocal. The asylum letter writers are characterized by *captatio benevolentiae* (from *ars dictaminis*: striving for benevolence), whereby they attempt wholeheartedly to inspire the goodwill of the recipients. At least on the surface, the letter writers oblige and do not create discord while maintaining their hierarchical social roles.

I now turn to the letters themselves.

Letters To Mrs. Thornton

The first group consists of twenty-three letters written by Superintendent Wilbur, the asylum matron, the steward, and two teachers (L. Hutchinson and L. L. Weld) to Mrs. Mary Thornton of Cincinnatus (who in 1859 became Mrs. Mary Whead of Caton), New York, between 1855 and 1866 regarding her institutionalized son, Jimmy Thornton. The Special Collections at Syracuse University purchased this collection of letters in 2008 and called it *The James Thornton Correspondence*. One would think that a collection with such a title would proffer instructive examples of letters written by James Thornton that elucidate some, any, experiences of his life. But these letters were not written by James (also called "Jamie" and "Jimmy"), nor do they elucidate detailed particulars of his experience. Rather, in the letters there is no indication of Jimmy's point of view, though I can partially reconstruct the point of view of his mother. The twenty-three extant letters—barring the first letter, in which Superintendent Wilbur requests Mrs. Thornton's name and address (notably strangely after Jimmy has already arrived at the institution)—are responses to the petitions made by Jimmy's mother. But Mrs. Thornton's petitions themselves are missing—absent from the historical record. Letters written by Mrs. Thornton to the asylum, as well as any other letters written by family members of pupils (except for letters excerpted in the institution's annual reports) appear to no longer exist. (I was unable not only to locate Mrs. Thornton's part of the correspondence, but also to pinpoint how *The James Thornton Correspondence* made its way into the Syracuse University Special Collections; the dealer who sold the collection to the university in 2008 had bought it from another dealer who could not recall how he had come to possess the letters, nearly sixteen years earlier).

Because of these and other gaps in the written record, instead of asking what writings by pupils and their families were left to us, I ask what we can infer based on the inscriptions and writings that survive. How can the pupils (Jimmy) and their families (Mrs. Thornton) be made part of the historical record without a breadth of evidence indicating their perspective? We must acknowledge that even though the pupils' and families' speaking, writing, and experience generally were not preserved, the absence of their words evokes an undeniable presence. I give a brief overview of what I found in the written record of *The James Thornton Correspondence*. Subsequently, I discuss what is there that is not to be found in the writing—the silent rhetoric and endless possibilities for creating presence.

A Timeline of James Thornton

1848: James Thornton is born in Cincinnatus, New York

1855: "Jimmy" enters the asylum at Syracuse; he is seven years old. The transition is difficult.

1859: Mary Thornton, Jimmy's mother, remarries and becomes Mrs. Whead.[10] She requests that he *not* be sent home.

1861: Dr. Wilbur sends Jimmy to Elmira, where he is met and taken home, at the asylum's expense.

1862: Dr. Wilbur writes to ask, "What has become of Jimmy Thornton?" No response is evident.

1865: James W. Thornton is listed on the Steuben County, N.Y. (Caton), census: age seventeen and living at home.

1870: Jimmy is listed on the census as living at home with his mother.

1880: Jimmy and his mother live alone in Caton, N.Y.; Jimmy is not listed as employed. Mary, his mother, is listed as widowed (Census Records).

1891: Presumably after his mother's death, one James Thornton resides at the Caton County Poorhouse. He is said to be suffering from "St. Vitus Dance."

1895: A James Thornton is sent to Williard State Hospital, then "sent to Rome." There he might have been institutionalized at the Rome State Custodial Asylum or the State School for the Deaf at Rome (Annual Proceedings of Steuben County).

We can learn from the letters that Jimmy Thornton was probably seven years old when he entered the asylum-school at Syracuse in September 1855. We know that he would have been one of the very first pupils in the new building at Syracuse after the asylum moved from Albany in 1854. We know that Dr. R. H. Gray of Cincinnatus, New York, most likely wrote the letter of application for Jimmy's admittance, as the first letter in the collection was written to Dr. Gray by Dr. Wilbur requesting the name and address of the mother of "the little boy from Cincinnatus." Jimmy's mother was Mrs. Mary Thornton, also from Cincinnatus, who became Mrs. Mary Whead when she remarried in 1859 and then moved farther away from the asylum, to Caton, New York. We presume that this must have influenced her relationship with her son and her relationship to the asylum, as we can observe a marked change in circumstances beginning around 1859, which corresponds to Mrs. Thornton's remarriage and her request that Jimmy *not* visit home. We learn from the letters that Jimmy Thornton was deaf, did not speak, knew some version of sign language (ASL as we know it had not yet been formalized), and read and wrote in English (Letter Fourteen).[11] We can guess that he attended the school as a state-funded pupil,[12] indicating that his mother was too poor to pay for his schooling (New York State had passed a free, public Common School law in 1812).

Even after his mother's remarriage in 1859, it appears that Jimmy continued on as a state-funded pupil (rather than the family's paying for his institutionalization), since there is no indication in the letters that his status changed.[13] I cannot ascertain Mrs. Thornton's financial status before or after remarriage, nor can I determine the ways in which her remarriage and relocation farther away from the asylum-school affected her relationship with Jimmy and with the asylum's administration. We know the man Jimmy's mother remarried was Mr. Thomas Whead (b. 1800), and that she herself was born in 1813. On the 1865 Census Record from Caton, New York, a brother is listed as Richard H. Thornton, age twenty-four. We also know that Jimmy left behind no samples of his own writing, not even any inscriptions, even though he is said to have been able to write a "good copy." This raises the question as to whether or not he would have written any original compositions or self-authored pieces, a question for which no answer is provided in the letters. Jimmy was given reasonable access to basic bilingual literacy education—in fact, reading and writing in English was a priority in deaf education across the United States (Edwards, 31, 38). While the letters document that he learned to write English and use sign language, it is significant that in the historical record, although he remains silent, he is not absent.

The first letter, dated September 7, 1855, is from Superintendent Wilbur to Dr. Gray, the authorizing physician from the town in which the Thorntons lived. The letter signals an initial intent of reassurance and consolation, though brief, and indicates the potentiality of the asylum's new acquisition, referred to anonymously as "the little boy from Cincinnatus." Dr. Wilbur begins his letter to Dr. Gray reassuring him that the boy has arrived and is well:

> Dear Sir,
>
> The little boy from Cincinnatus is very well and quite at home and contented with us. I think that he will make a very good pupil. If you will please to write to me giving the name and P.O. address of the mother—I will write to her occasionally of her child's welfare.
>
> Yours Truly
>
> H. B. Wilbur (Letter One)

As in this first letter, throughout the correspondence letter writers from the asylum avoided entirely the medicalized labels and phrases of the time such as *idiot*, *destitute*, *unfortunates*, or *feeble-minded*. Entirely different from the rhetoric used by the institution that I have discussed in chapter 3, the letters attempted to console and reassure the families who had just lost their sons or daughters by erasing references to the feared "idiot asylum"; instead, the letter writers ushered in an illusion of an idyllic home away from home where the treasured student (in this case, Jimmy) could grow into a man. Asylum letter writers, unlike the family letter writers discussed later, avoided use of deficiency-based observations by deploying lines of argument related to benevolence, praise, progress, goodwill, and sentimentalism. Wilbur's reference in Letter One to the fact that Jimmy was "at home" would be reiterated in the bulk of the letters as a way to assuage and console the family for any regret they felt at having sent the child away. The letters continually refashioned the asylum into an intimate household that cared for the "well-being" of its charges and replaced the "real" family home.[14]

The "boy" discussed in Letter One remained nameless even though the school had only between fifty and sixty students in 1855—the trope of anonymity was at work (see chapter 2). Wilbur promised Dr. Gray that he would "occasionally" write to "the boy's mother" (also nameless) to inform her of "her child's welfare." In Letter One, Mary Thornton was "the child's mother" rather than "Jimmy's mother," since Wilbur had no knowledge of the family's, or even Jimmy's, name. This was uncommon (but not entirely atypical for the time period) to have a child arrive in this anonymous fashion with nothing more than an admittance form sent ahead by a doctor. This letter from Wilbur to Dr. Gray, acknowledging the boy's admittance, is brief—a total of three sentences in which an assurance of the boy's well-being comes first followed by a simple request for the family's (and the boy's) name. The letter is direct and to the point: Wilbur desires only a name and address to attach to the "little" body that has thus entered his school. We have no way of knowing exactly why Jimmy arrived in this fashion, who brought him to the asylum-school, what method of transportation was used to convey him, or whether anyone understood his "home signs." Notwithstanding these unknowns, this first letter demonstrates a dynamic that will continue throughout the correspondence, in which harmony and benevolence are couched in bureaucratic brevity: amid directness and concision, the letter expresses no displeasure or discord regarding any part of the process of arrival, admittance, and anonymity.

Letter Two, undated[15] and written by E. F. Mulford, the matron of the asylum,[16] offers more reassurance, though it is a reassurance that would not come directly to Mrs. Thornton but rather through an intermediary who had come to the asylum to gather news on Jimmy and report back to the family. In the letter, Matron Mulford consoles Mrs. Thornton with a brief description of Jimmy's experience:

> I hope you will hear [through the intermediary] a favorable account of your boy's progress and feel satisfied that he remembers you for really I was quite surprised to see him show so much emotion—he

> actually shed tears. But this gentleman who is the bearer of this will tell you all.
>
> From The Matron Mrs. E. F. Mulford

In this letter, the matron refers to the arrival at the asylum of what must have been a family friend who called in order to inquire on behalf of Mrs. Thornton. The letter tells us that Jimmy shed tears at the memory of his mother. We can infer that for any number of reasons it would have been difficult for Mrs. Thornton to visit her son herself. It is possible that her first husband had died and, as a woman, Mrs. Thornton could not have easily traveled alone. Possibly she did not have the money or the time to make the trip from Cincinnatus to Syracuse, which was a journey of forty-three miles. In 1855, only the larger towns in central New York, such as Syracuse, Albany, and Rochester, were connected by the New York Central Railroad. The Erie Canal went only east and west, not south where Mrs. Thornton lived. If she had had the money, felt safe traveling alone, and could get time off from work (if she worked), Mrs. Thornton still would have had to go to Syracuse and return by horse-drawn carriage or wagon, which would have taken three days each way. This letter from Matron Mulford offers the first of many indications that Mrs. Thornton did not have easy access to her son. This fact forced her to rely on letters as the most accessible mode of gathering information.

Harmony and Accord

Amid what must have been a difficult experience for both mother and son, the letter writers from the asylum consistently put forth a formal display of goodwill toward Jimmy, who is consistently praised as the treasured pupil, a jewel of a student whose bodily, behavioral, and intellectual presence, as it is rehabilitated, brings joy to the entire asylum. This goodwill is extended to Jimmy's family, and though it is possible to assume, it is difficult to know for certain whether the asylum's staff sincerely cared about Jimmy Thornton. A year into Jimmy's schooling, Superintendent Wilbur reassures Mrs. Thornton:

> Your little boy continues well—he is perfectly happy in his new home and getting on nicely in school matters. He is an affectionate little fellow and all the teachers and attendants are quite attracted to him. (Letter Five, November 20, 1855)

Wilbur's assistant, and the school steward, H. H. Saville, goes on to console the family in another letter a year later. As Saville writes, Wilbur did not have enough time to write to all the families, so Saville wrote for him:

> Your little boy is perfectly well and very well supplied with clothes. He appears perfectly contented and his teachers like him very much. Indeed he is a favorite with everybody in the Asylum. (Letter Seven, September 1, 1856)

Wilbur and his staff discursively manifest the impression that all is well. The two letters above repeat lines of argument designed to reassure and console Mrs. Thornton that her son is well liked and acclimating successfully to his new "home." The letters have an undercurrent that appears intended to encourage Mrs. Thornton to endure the distance between herself and her son. In Letter Seven, as Wilbur was again too busy to write, Saville continues to console and reassure:

> I hope you feel quite easy about him for he seems healthy and he is much more in the way of improvement here than could possibly be at home.
>
> Your Truly H. H. Saville for Dr. H. B. Wilbur (Letter Seven, September 1, 1856)

Throughout all of the twenty-three letters, Jimmy is said to be "very well" (x2), "very happy" (x3), "well and happy" (x2), "very well and happy" (x3), "very happy here now," "very well and quite at home," "perfectly well and enjoys himself," "continues well" (x2), "continues very well," "perfectly well and very well," "moreover happy and contented," and "quite well and never unhappy." These repetitions of terms of "wellness" were undoubtedly designed to reinforce the conception that Jimmy was well and contented in his new home. They could as well have reflected the benign intention on the part of Wilbur and his staff to assuage Mrs. Thornton's regrets for sending her son away. Also, it is possible that Jimmy was doing really well and the asylum wished to convey that fact to his mother. Or maybe this was simply a discursive convention—a standard reassurance—used in all letters, which acted as a sort of methodical incantation.

Tension and Discordance

What becomes apparent in these letters, and most instructive, is the extent to which this demonstration of goodwill and this reporting of only what was concordant could have functioned as some sort of epistolary and bureaucratic artifice as Jimmy's stay at the institution lengthened. After noting such an overwhelming level of polite manners in the letters, I began to ask myself: Is there anything beneath the artifice? What's not being recorded? This is to say that the goodwill on the part of Wilbur and the asylum staff toward Jimmy and Mrs. Thornton was certainly in some sense sincere—they certainly cared about him and *believed* that they were doing what was best for him, for society, and for his family. Yet an irreconcilable tension lies in the fact that what is absent in the discourse of these letters from the asylum is any acknowledgment of discord or nonacquiescence. In sifting through the layers of rhetoric, the family's experience and perspective emerge, perhaps not surprisingly, as being at least potentially at odds with the experience and perspective of the asylum. Mrs. Thornton was in no way overtly resistant to institutionalization; she might have, at least initially, conceived of the asylum-school as a haven that took from her the "burden" of caring for Jimmy, in a time when society offered few support services.

Nevertheless, I can evoke traces of Mrs. Thornton's presence in several ways. The letter writers at the asylum were anything but thorough and forthcoming in their reports to Mrs. Thornton, and undoubtedly this left her with unanswered questions. Wilbur and others sometimes were slightly dismissive, and in their brevity and concision with Mrs. Thornton (evident in references to how little time they had for writing) behaved in ways that she might have found disconcerting. And there must have been times when Mrs. Thornton expressed a desire to visit Jimmy and/or have him come home.

One trace of Mrs. Thornton's perspective comes during discussion of her desire to visit Jimmy. In Letter Three, we can surmise that the gentle, advisory tone Superintendent Wilbur uses is a response to some expression of nonaccommodation or displeasure by Mrs. Thornton, which she had communicated in a prior (no longer extant) letter to him. In his letter, Wilbur advises her not to visit her son. He writes, six months into Jimmy's stay:

> He will be very glad to see you—though for the present, a visit from you might make him homesick again. (Letter Three, October 8, 1855)

The letter then ends abruptly, "Yours in haste, H. B. Wilbur." It is not illogical to suppose that in this short letter Wilbur might have been responding to Mrs. Thornton's request to visit her son, and that the asylum's answer reflects his concern that a visit from Jimmy's mother might hinder "the boy's" chance of becoming "an excellent pupil." It is possible that Wilbur was concerned that Jimmy would want to leave the asylum with his mother if she visited, while it is also possible that Wilbur did not want Jimmy to "regress" in his adjustment to his new home and therefore was managing Jimmy, and "handling" Mrs. Thornton, out of a sincere desire to see Jimmy succeed in his educational programming, which included a difficult period of adjustment to a new life. Or perhaps, as an entirely different scenario,

Mrs. Thornton had communicated that she could *not* come for a visit at this time, and Wilbur, then, was trying to console her for not being able to come.

Mrs. Thornton must have written back to Wilbur shortly after what might have been either a slight admonition or an attempt at consolation, and in her letter she might have again appeared discordant with the situation. Wilbur's response was posted two weeks after Mrs. Thornton's request to visit, during what constituted the most intensive period of correspondence (the most letters back and forth in the shortest time frame). The letter reads as follows:

> Dear Madam,
>
> I have but little time to write letters and many letters to write, so that I have to write short letters to all the friends of my pupils. Your little boy is very happy here now. He is very desirous of learning and will in time make an excellent pupil. He is a favorite with all, as I think, I wrote you before.
>
> Yours truly H. B. Wilbur (Letter Four, October 22, 1855)

Perhaps this attempt by Wilbur to further reassure Mrs. Thornton was not successful, or was mitigated by his hasty closing. On the other hand, it is possible that she was content with Wilbur's response and in the end felt comfortable with what appears to have been a decision to deny her a visit. Or, perhaps Mrs. Thornton continued to be troubled by the fact that she may have been advised against visiting her son. In the letter, Wilbur's language is more curt than in the other letters—he indicates Jimmy's progress and suitability for the school program with slight irritation and impatience at having to repeat the information. It is possible that his impatience grew as Mrs. Thornton continued to request more information and as she likely felt the growing distance between herself and her son, as well as a growing sense of not being able to participate in her son's life.

We can identify repetition in asylum rhetoric in which little or no new information on Jimmy is furnished and instead consolation and reassurance appear somewhat superfluous, rushed, and mechanical. Wilbur likely had little time to attend any more to Mrs. Thornton's resentment at not being able to visit or remain intimate with her son, although that did not mean that he did not care. Rather, Wilbur's rhetoric in Letter Four indicates an accumulation of evidence that depicts Mrs. Thornton through the layering of perspective as having unanswered questions and continued concerns, the nature of which we can never be certain of.

In the succeeding three years' worth of correspondence there is little space to sift through the layering in search of more traces of her perspective. Letters written between 1856 and 1859 number seven, and the asylum letter writers range from H. H. Saville (the steward) and E. F. Mulford (the matron) to L. Hutchinson (Jimmy's teacher). Wilbur himself did not communicate with Mrs. Thornton for these three-plus years, which probably indicates that no extraordinary situations involving Jimmy occurred, for if something dire had happened it is likely that he would have written (the entire epistolary tells us that Wilbur or his wife stepped into the conversation whenever something was amiss or a situation required special attention). The letters written by Saville, Mulford, and Hutchinson (Letters Seven to Fourteen) perform work similar to Wilbur's initial letters, which addressed Mrs. Thornton's regret for sending her son away. While Saville's letters (Seven and Eight) mimic the diction and content of Wilbur's previous letters nearly perfectly, the letters written by Mulford and, less so, Hutchinson are the most detailed in that both letter writers present anecdotes to illustrate particular things Jimmy has done at the asylum-school or give specific details with regard to how he is faring. For example, in Letter Nine, Matron Mulford writes,

> He came in our dining room and took dinner with the family on Sunday noon. He was somewhat nervous but still enjoyed it very much. He is a sweet affectionate child and a general favorite. We made him understand that he with the other children are to have a fine time Christmas—we always devote our undivided attention to their amusement on that day and the Dr. will make them all some little present—Jamie has sufficient clothing for the winter—do not give yourself the least [illegible] for my assistant takes the best care of him. He always kisses me a sweet goodnight.
>
> Yours resp'ly E. F. Mulford

Perhaps she was more detailed in her reports than Saville or Wilbur because Mulford was engaged in the everyday routine of the pupils. In the following letter, Mulford also apologizes, as Saville had, for Wilbur's absence as the letter writer. She too repeats terms of "wellness":

> Again the Dr. has availed himself of my services in the letter writing department. I can only say that your boy is well, happy, and doing well in school. . . . I have many letters to write and must hasten from one to another.
>
> Briefly but sincerely yours E. F. Mulford (Letter Ten)

In Letter Eleven, Mulford gives the most detailed report yet of Jimmy's progress in schooling:

> He is a darling boy and he improves so much in school—is so easily managed. He can put up a great many words on the letter board and read almost any word on the blackboard. He is perfectly well and enjoys himself—We have more than one hundred pupils and but one case of sickness.
>
> Yours in haste E. F. Mulford (Letter Eleven)

Like Mulford's letters, L. Hutchinson's (Jimmy's teacher) letters demonstrate that she observed Jimmy firsthand and worked with him daily. Her first letter is brief (Letter Thirteen), essentially attesting that he is a good pupil, is well, and is in good health. Her following letters (Letters Fourteen and Fifteen) offer more educational information. Hutchinson writes:

> He seems very much delighted with any exercise and perhaps it would be gratifying to you to know that. I consider him one of the best pupils under my charge. He can write any thing with a copy before him and a great many words and sentences without [copy]. He is also learning to read but slowly of course because you know he is deaf and dumb and obliged to be taught wholly by signs.
>
> Yours Respectfully,
>
> L. Hutchinson (Letter Fourteen)

Hutchinson wrote only three letters. Her correspondence may have been severed due to the end of the school year in 1859, when most of the teachers left and only the Wilbur family and a few employees remained.

Letter Fifteen is the first letter addressed to Mrs. Whead and signifies a shift in the correspondence. Letter Fifteen not only utilizes Jimmy's mother's new name (which indicates her remarriage) but also is the first written by Harriet (H. H.) Wilbur, Superintendant Wilbur's wife. We cannot know why Mrs. Wilbur became the letter writer in January 1859, but it is possible that asylum employees had left on a winter vacation and that Superintendent Wilbur gave her the responsibility of writing to families. Mrs. Wilbur is again the letter writer later that same year (Letter Sixteen, July 10, 1859), and again we can infer that either no one else had remained at the asylum during the summer who could write to the families or the situation that had to be reported was dire enough to necessitate a letter from Harriet in lieu of her husband, who, she tells us, was out of town (Letter Fifteen).

In the letter, dated July 15, 1859, Harriet adamantly attempts to persuade Mrs. Whead to send for her son so that Jimmy will not have to stay on at the asylum through the summer vacation (Letter Sixteen, July 15, 1859). Mrs. Wilbur writes,

> The annual vacation of the Asylum commences on the Monday of next July 18th instant. Your son is very desirous of going home and Dr. Wilbur wishes me to say that he wishes it also. You will please reply to this *immediately* and state when you will come or send for him.

This constitutes a shift because not only are Jimmy's wishes voiced ("Your son is desirous of going home"), but an attempt is being made to carry them out. But Mrs. Whead must have replied by requesting that Jimmy stay on at the asylum through the summer of 1859—at which point Mrs. Wilbur responds,

> Dr. Wilbur wishes me to say in reply to the letter of yours of date of July 25, that your son can remain through the vacation. He is very well. (Letter Seventeen)

We have no way of knowing why Mrs. Whead might have requested that her son stay at the asylum through the summer. It is possible that she may not have preferred that he stay but could not, for any number of reasons, allow him to return home at that time. It is possible that she feared that he would lose his "hard-to-come-by" spot as a pupil, or that she simply could not manage her son's return home due to adverse financial, emotional, or other unforeseeable circumstances in her life. Perhaps her new husband did not wish Jimmy to return.

What we do know is that Mrs. Wilbur does not append the conventional closing to this abbreviated response to Mrs. Whead; instead, she offers only her signature. This is a fraught moment: here, Mrs. Whead's words might be imagined to have an uncanny sense, in that her words, from the perspective of a contemporary reader, would seem uncomfortably strange and unexpected. In the absence of any evidence, we can only guess that she replied to Harriet Wilbur asking, "Can he indeed remain on through the summer?" We have no way of knowing if she did indeed write this and, if so, what the circumstances were that led to the request. And, more importantly, Jimmy's wishes do not appear to have been part of either the asylum's or his mother's considerations.

The next letter (Letter Eighteen) was written nearly two years later (March 1861). This was the longest period without correspondence, which suggests that Mrs. Whead's request to have him stay on through the summer of 1859 may have somehow had larger repercussions for everyone. This letter illustrates the battle that was waged between the asylum and the family over who crossed over the border between the asylum and the community and when that border could be crossed. Again, the asylum encourages Jimmy to leave. In July 1861 Dr. Wilbur was again the letter writer, which indicates the possible urgency of the situation. This was another turning point in the correspondence, in which Jimmy's departure from the asylum-school was set in motion. Wilbur writes,

> Mrs. Whead, Dear Madam,
>
> Should you like to have your son Jimmy come home if I would send him to Elmira without expense to you? Would you meet him there and like him home, if I would write you? It would do him much good to go home.
>
> Yours Truly H. B. Wilbur

It is probable that Jimmy had not returned home for the entire six years he had remained enrolled at the asylum-school; moreover, there is evidence of only one possible visit from Mrs. Whead during that time. But it was this belated gesture by Wilbur to finance Jimmy's trip home that allowed him to leave. If Wilbur could send Jimmy to Elmira (near Caton, where she had relocated after remarriage), Mrs. Whead could easily pick up her son there. So home Jimmy went for the first time in six years, on a five-day journey to Elmira and then Caton in the summer of 1861. It appears that the asylum sent Jimmy home thinking that he would return to the asylum after his visit to Caton.

But six months after James Thornton left the asylum, in January 1862, he still had not returned to Syracuse. Four years later, Jimmy still had not returned, and (as far as we can tell) no word had been received from Mrs. Whead. On January 8, 1866, Dr. Wilbur communicated in his final letter with what seems near-desperation. As if to demonstrate how the dynamics and lines of argument had shifted once the pupil/inmate had left the institution, it is Wilbur who pleads for information, Wilbur himself who took the time to write,

> Is [Jimmy] still living? What is his state of health? How has he grown? What does he do and how does he amuse himself? Does he ever speak of his life here? We were talking about him the other day, and I cannot resist the desire to hear from him once more. Please

write me about him. . . . What has become of Jimmy Thornton, as we used to call him?

I remain yours truly, H. B. Wilbur.

This letter demonstrates a remarkable shift that deviates from the bureaucratic incantations of many of the earlier letters. And, thus, we are left contemplating the same sincere question: What *did* become of Jimmy Thornton?

More than nine years after he left the asylum, the 1870 census and, ten years later, the 1880 census showed Jimmy "at home" (not working) with his mother—in 1870, his stepfather Thomas Wheat (likely, a mispelling) was seventy and his mother was fifty-four. By 1880, Mary Whead was sixty-four and widowed, and the report shows that the she was living alone with Jimmy, who would have been thirty-two years of age. Sometime after that, it appears that Mrs. Thornton/Whead died, since Jimmy became a dependent of the county. The 1890 federal census of Caton, New York, was lost in an archive fire, but the 1891 and 1895 Annual Proceedings of the Steuben County Board of Supervisors state that a James Thornton, suffering from "St. Vitus Dance" (loss of motor control brought on by rheumatic fever), resided in the county poor house in 1891. In 1895, a James Thornton appears to have been a patient at Willard State Hospital for "lunacy" for part of the year, and in the same year a James Thornton was "sent to Rome"—the New York State School for the Deaf at Rome, New York, which had been established in the 1870s by a deaf educator.

Listening Further

We can learn from this correspondence that the border between the asylum and the rest of the world, not surprisingly, was tightly controlled, although, ironically, in the most familiar, cordial, and seemingly friendly ways. We know that in 1855 Mrs. Thornton sent her son Jimmy to the asylum-school at Syracuse at the behest of a physician, that thereafter she lost control over visitation, and that he did not return home until the asylum financed his journey, in 1861. We can deduce that the relationship between Mrs. Thornton (later, Mrs. Whead) and the asylum was influenced by her financial resources and that the balance of power between them shifted once Jimmy left the institution; after Jimmy left, it was the asylum-school that expressed a sense of distress at not knowing what had become of him. We can conclude that when Jimmy left the asylum the family gained back, at the very least, communicative power—Mrs. Whead no longer petitioned for information, no longer received incomplete reports, and no longer was told what was best for Jimmy. We also know that having returned to his home he did not reenter the asylum-school, nor did his family write to offer an update. This final silence might have indicated defiance. Or, it could have been something else entirely.

In "The Doubting Dance," Phil Ferguson invites us to "fill out the historical record of how parents of earlier eras described their experiences" (2), and these letters do point us in that direction. Close study of both the rhetoric and the silences found in the letters indicates the difficulties Mrs. Thornton experienced in her relationship with the asylum-school. The letters show us that even in the very early years of asylum-schools, before mass institutionalization emerged, resistance by families was more complicated and insidious than we think. From the evidence of these asylum letters, we can appreciate more deeply the frustration Mrs. Thornton must have experienced in her attempts to gain information about her child, and the difficulties occasioned by being without him for so long. But still, one character is left silent—Jimmy himself. Nonetheless, this correspondence demonstrates the complexity of the emotions that surrounded the plight of people who were institutionalized and their families—and the position of people with disabilities whose fate was entirely determined by forces beyond their control.

Letters from Families and Pupils: In Praise of the Institution

The second set of letters, written not by the asylum but by families and pupils themselves, is similar to the first set of letters written to Mrs. Thornton in that they also serve, in the most seemingly benevolent way, to validate Dr. Wilbur and the work of the asylum. Here the letter writers are the pupils and their siblings, parents, and advocates. This is especially interesting because the social hierarchies are altogether maintained.[17] No resistance to institutionalization, and no discordance, exists that we can see. Perhaps families did not resist institutionalization, or they considered institutionalization their best option; they also might have appreciated the ways in which institutions relieved them of the difficulty of caring for someone, during a time when they would have received little or no support at home. All that is left in the written record of this asylum-school (as far as my research has revealed to me) are the family and pupil letters that were displayed by Wilbur at exhibitions and in the annual reports to the New York Legislature. These efforts by Dr. Wilbur to display letters of praise for his work were intended to legitimize the asylum in the estimation of state officials, funders, and the public.

The letters (ten in total) from this second set must be read bearing in mind that that they were selected, edited, prepared, and then displayed by Dr. Wilbur in reports to the state legislature between 1853 and 1867. I have selected the first eight letters from the asylum's annual reports; the last two were displayed at the Pan American Exposition in Buffalo in 1893. It is evident in view of the contexts in which they were displayed that their main function was to persuade both the legislative body and (at the Exposition) the public that the families served by the institution believed that the asylum was legitimate, successful, and fulfilled a much-needed, even lifesaving function. That the letters were included in the annual reports or displayed at the Pan American Exposition ultimately means that they depicted points of view that argued on behalf of the institution.

Additionally, while *The James Thornton Correspondence* contains progress reports and responses to petitions in the expression of which the institution seems to wield most if not all of the leverage (until they no longer have charge of Jimmy), the eight letters I have extracted from annual reports between 1853 and 1867 (six from the report of 1866) demonstrate strategies that give a nod from "below" to the institution's authority. These letters from the families to the asylum all defer to the asylum's authority, in respectful attitudes that may have assisted them in their attempts to gain admittance or maintain a spot for their children. As Poster and Lipson posit, awareness of social rank comes to be an important function for people attempting to negotiate from a weaker social position (Lipson, 87–92; Poster, 37). The eight letters from the annual reports appease and accommodate institutional authority by offering evidence of the institution's success. We can look to this second set of letters to see intense deference communicated by families.

In the letters, the families petitioned for information about their children with near desperation, due to the children's prolonged absence. The families were in desperate need of information. Each letter reflects a family's position in which they were utterly dependent on the institution until their child was no longer a pupil there; after the pupil had left the asylum-school, according to the evidence selected for publication by Wilbur, his or her family was grateful. The letter writers needed something from the asylum and therefore were forced to demonstrate deference in order to assure the family's petition would be answered. Letter Twenty-Four (1853) written to the asylum from John's sister, Lucy G., expresses the desperation of her desire for news of John's progress. She writes,

> To John's Teacher:
>
> Excuse us for we are unknown to your name. We hope you will be kind enough to answer us as soon as this reaches you, as we are very anxious to hear from John. . . . I think you had better write a letter to us about John, instead of Dr. Wilbur, because he may be

> engaged in his business. We wish to know what John does in school, and wish you to tell us about him particularly. . . . I expect that my father will go to Albany on a visit next spring. Does he [John] have a mind to learn? Tell John that my mother gives a great deal of love to him. We wish to know if he feels homesick, and does he love to learn? Please ask if he remembers all our names, and what town we live in? Has John grown any since he left our home and went to school, or has his appearance changed? (Letter Twenty-Four, 1853)

One interpretation of this is that the letter writer, Lucy G., is pleading for detailed and specific information rather than the generic report the family had probably received from Dr. Wilbur previously (similar to the brief and redundant reports Mrs. Thornton received). Lucy G. is deferential and grateful but also anxious, and begs for answers to her questions, assuming that the family will receive a more detailed account of John's progress from the teacher than they would from Wilbur. Another possibility is that Lucy had already asked these questions in an earlier letter and received no response, which might account for her anxious tone. Or perhaps the family had become distanced from John of their own accord and had not corresponded with the asylum for a while, which would explain her desperate tone a bit differently.

Desperation appears again in a letter from a father who writes to beg for his daughter's admittance. He relates in detail that the family may be forced out of their tenement house because their "unfortunate" and "unhappy" child frightens the neighbors with her "constant mischief" and her playing with fire. The father offers his plea:

> Our desire to place her under the charge of such a one as you . . . and be you to advise me as soon as convenient, whether and when you will be ready to grant our wish of seeing her placed in your excellent institution, With the assurance of my deepest respect,— (Letter Thirty-One, 1867)

This expression "of my deepest respect" demonstrates more deference for the asylum than can be found in any of the Thornton letters written by the asylum to families. To strengthen his plea, and demonstrate the urgency of his situation, the father utilizes the language of deficiency. The child is characterized as "unhappy" and "unfortunate," and is such a "heavy charge upon us."

In their letters, many of the other families also utilize the language of deficiency, which counterbalances what they acknowledge as the asylum's "great" works. Whereas *The James Thornton Correspondence*, consisting of letters from the institution to the families, only mentions positive progress and potential, the families consistently deploy the language of deficiency. Another instance of the language of deficiency is seen in Letter Twenty-Five (1866), regarding W. C.; the letter, rather than petitioning for information or admittance, is a thank you letter to Wilbur and his staff for engaging in "the ungrateful task of educating an unfortunate class." The letter of appreciation and acknowledgment is from a prominent banker who uses the language of deficiency to establish the state of his child as an antithesis to the praiseworthy work the school performs. The banker expresses pleasure in seeing the child's improvement from having a "morbid appetite" to being able to read and write self-sufficiently.

Another letter (1866) regards J. O. and was written by his father. This is the most commanding of all the family letters. J. O.'s father must have felt he shared social rank with Wilbur. The letter includes unwavering, almost ornate, praise of the change that the asylum has impressed upon his son. Impassioned gratitude as well as the language of deficiency can be seen here as the father writes,

> I had intended to have written you at an earlier date, to express my hearty appreciation of your labors, and those of your co-laborers for the benefit of my unfortunate son, who is under your care. I have at no time hoped for his entire recovery, because I could not expect the entire eradication of his physical disease, which superinduced the mental weakness and deranged conditions of his mind and his actions. Up to the time that the scrofula, which was fastened upon him by vaccination, he evinced as sprightly and harmonious mental conditions as any child of the same age. The delirium, which manifested itself when he was about twenty months or two years old, remained as you saw him when he first came to your institution. The occasional and disconnected sallies of wit and understanding which he evinces, shows that his original mental power has not been wholly destroyed, but clouded and confused by the morbid condition and action of his cerebral organs. In placing him under your care it was in the hope that by a training adapted to his condition—one such as with my duties I could not give, and is not found in any ordinary schooling for youth—that the latent mind might be aroused, and so far regulated in its actions that he might, should he live, be a comfort to us and to himself. I am highly gratified by his success thus far. (Letter Twenty-Seven, 1866)

The letter demonstrates the amount of detail family letters often proffered to the asylum, in contrast to the minimal detail and formulaic reporting families received from the asylum. J. O's father writes about the improvements he has seen in areas of health, physicality, behavior, aptitude, etc. The letter is much more impassioned, detailed, and engaged than any of the progress reports written from the asylum. This is not surprising but it is nonetheless significant in that the amount of detail and level of engagement measure the difference in the relative social positions of the writers of the letters.

While the letters from the asylum offer few if any details regarding the pupils, the families supply more in their reports on the pupils' progress after they have left the school (as seen, for example, in the letter from J. O's father). These reports (Letters Twenty-Seven, Twenty-Eight, Twenty-Nine, 1866) do not include the desperate tone of some of the others, because in these examples the family no longer requires anything from the institution; rather, they are writing to inform and to give thanks. One letter, included with Case no. 14 (referred to as P. S) offers numerous evaluative details of P. S.'s successful employment as a day laborer for the railroad:

> He is at present working upon the railroad track as a day laborer. He receives $1.25 per day, and boards with his mother. He is very steady, and works intelligently—i.e. understands what he is told to do, and does it. He appears to be willing to work, and works when not prevented by stormyweather. His wages amount to more than is required for his support, and therefore must be some help to his mother. (Letter Twenty-Eight, 1866)

Just as *The Thornton Correspondence* was laden with the language of goodwill, these letters from family members and friends that have been selected and excerpted for the annual reports highly praise the institution.

What is more interesting in the letters written by families is that there are a few salient instances in which the letter writers refer to the pupils' voices. Though Mrs. Wilbur does refer to Jimmy's wish to go home (in *The Thornton Letters*), she does not quote him, nor do any other of the letter writers from the asylum. Perhaps most significant is that we learn that Jimmy had learned to write, but for some reason he did not write to his mother. In contrast, included in one of the family letters (Letter Thirty, 1866) is a report by E. S.'s mother that communicates her son's message to the asylum staff after he has left. She writes,

> He never spoke anything but kindness and love received while with you, and yet, said he, "I was lonesome here all the time," putting his hand on his heart.

But then E. S.'s mother confesses:

> There is but one unpleasant association connected with his stay with you and that is his baths; he always speaks of them with a shudder. He wants me to send his love to yourself and family, all the teachers and others connected with the institution. What is to be the future of our boy, is still a mystery; but we shall ever feel very grateful to all connected with the institution, for their kindness to him.
>
> Yours, truly

E. S.'s voice is most identifiable in this letter, wherein E. S. has asked his mother to write in order to tell everyone at the asylum that he will visit "once he becomes a man." E. S.'s mother feels the need to reassure the asylum and its staff that nothing bad had happened that influenced this decision to not return to live there; in fact, the inclusion of this "one unpleasant association" (in an annual report) is noteworthy because this comment might be taken to imply that, although the rhetoric of the letters demonstrates that the asylum-school strove to maintain an sir of constant tranquility or harmony, baths may have been a contentious activity that disrupted that harmony. The letters, however, do not refer to the circumstances mentioned by E. S.'s mother, whereby discordance might have arisen. This gap in information might have been filled by including more pupils' voices, but that would never have happened in the venue of the annual report (or in any other venue, for that matter).

Another letter (Letter Twenty-Six, 1866) alludes to the perspective and voice of the pupil. This is the only instance of a family member writing directly to a pupil. In the letter, F.'s mother asks him to thank the doctor and his staff "for the care and pains they take with thee." Acknowledging reading and intellectual ability on her son's part, F.'s mother writes,

> I am very happy to have the opportunity of replying to a letter by thee. It was a great surprise to me; was well written, well worded and gave me great courage that thee will one day be able to read and write as well as any of us.

The annual report in which the letter appears notes that the boy was "taken into the school room quite astonishing his teachers by his progress and his strong desire to learn" (1866 *Annual Report*, 44). After another term in the schoolroom, "with some labor and after two or three copyings, he wrote a letter home" (ibid.). The letter written by F. to his mother appears no longer to exist.

Any surviving words of the pupils themselves are few and far between. I was able to find only two texts (one is a letter), which were displayed at the 1893 Pan American Exposition in Buffalo. These two texts remain preserved in the New York State Archives, in the exact format of their display at the exposition. The asylum staff must have traveled to Buffalo in order to display their successes. The display of the texts exemplifies the way in which the pupil's "voice" or point of view was layered over by the voice of the staff. The first text (Letter Thirty-Two, 1893) was mounted on a cardboard display that had been divided into four sections. The top left panel reads as if introducing a medical case file:

> Letter, March 2, 1893 Class B-Subclass 1, no. 10-588.

Then the pupil's writing is pasted onto the panel:

> Dear Mother, I was glad to hear from you. I hope you had a nice time Christmas. Evelyn was going to send you a pin for Christmas and I was going to send you something but the things were so big they would not go in the letter. We have a good time here. We go out sleigh riding every day. I hope you will write to us soon.
>
> From your Loving Son D—

Following the pupil's writing is a medical evaluation, medical label, and institutional authorization:

> (Imbecile medium Grade, D. R. Age 9, 1892) . . . this boy has been in the institution thirteen months. When admitted he could not make a letter. He has had no assistance in writing this letter except in spelling some words.

The actual letter written by the pupil has been bookended by medicalized writing. Apparently, the letter was not thought to be worthy to stand alone.

Letter Thirty-Three (1893) is displayed in the same way on a cardboard panel divided into four sections. The bottom left of this next letter begins with the medical rhetoric and reads:

> Class B-Subclass 1, no. 10-588
>
> "Writing—Individual Progress"
>
> This low-grade imbecile girl entered the instit. in 1887 at the age of six. At the end of the first year she was trying to make an *e.*

> At the end of the second year she could make ten letters and a few simple words. She has continued to improve though slowly, till now she can make all the small and capitol letters and over two hundred words, and combine them in sentences without assistance.

Then, pasted at the top of the panel (not written directly on the cardboard like the staff's caption):

> I want to go home this summer and see my mother. She lives in New York. We can go up to the woods and pick flowers in the Spring.

This pupil has not been identified, even by initials; her writing sample is surrounded by her case and class number and by an institutional seal (on the back of each panel is the seal of the Syracuse State Institution for Feeble-Minded Children).[18]

These two examples of writing by pupils are instructive in that they show that pupils' writing was preserved only to display the successes of the institution. The first of the pupil texts/letters from "your loving son D." attempts to demonstrate how idyllic the asylum was. The second text, however, resonates in an uncanny way with the desire on the pupil's part to go home, if only for the summer. These two texts attempted to show the people who visited the display in 1893 in Buffalo that the asylum at Syracuse *could* teach the "idiot," as proven on these panels. These two texts are all that we have of the pupils' writing; they exemplify the ways in which nearly all of the letters preserved in the historical record of the asylum at Syracuse accommodated, praised, and celebrated the institution, the imaginable exceptions being those that might have been supplied by what I can hypothesize about Mrs. Thornton's, and others,' (non-extant) petitions. At best, then, on the basis of the historical record we can only surmise: If Jimmy Thornton had composed original writings, what *might* he have written?

Listening Even Further

Parts of the written historical record of the New York State Asylum have been so thoroughly erased that all we have been left with are examples of letters by pupils and families that appear one-sided in their expressions of satisfaction with the institution and its works. I was only able to locate two letters/texts written by the pupils themselves, a strangely insufficient sample when we consider that the purpose of curriculum of the school, as discussed in chapter 3, was to teach reading and writing. Why, out of more than five thousand pupils who attended between 1854 and 1884, do only two writing samples by pupils remain in the archive? How is it that only the family voices that support institutionalization remain? The harmonious and accommodating history told in the discourses of these letters is one-sided; surely it is not the whole story. What does a researcher do when anonymity and silence seem to be the dominating historiographic reality? To answer these questions, I look briefly to other letter writing within disability culture that accesses more direct subjectivity. While this chapter offers an extremely constrained access to the viewpoints of the pupils and families, because they were filtered through the institution, it is important that we locate the asylum letters in the context of letter writing more generally because to do so suggests the extent to which our methodologies do not account for those who did not write.

In "The Prisoner's Hidden Life, or Insane Asylums Unveiled," written in 1868, Elizabeth Parsons Ware Packard attested to the degradation and abuse that she herself had suffered while in the Illinois Mental Asylum at Jacksonville. She attached five other testimonies by women to her own; these narratives were included in the *Report of the Investigating Committee of the Legislature of Illinois*. Packard's narrative reversed the direction of the trope of the Described (discussed in chapter 2); rather than allowing herself to be the object of description by the institution, she described the institution's conditions and practices. But in the asylum letters from Syracuse (also selected for the legislature to view), we can find no descriptions of conditions of confinement in the letters except those that are idyllic, comforting, and family-like. A significant difference between Packard's ability to self-describe and the same ability as it existed among the pupils from the asylum-school can be explained by the fact that people with mental illness confined in mental asylums typically were treated differently in terms of their intelligence than people in "idiot" asylums. Historically, people diagnosed with mental illness had more access to literacy, whereby people with developmental disabilities did not gain access to literacy until later in the twentieth century.[19]

Like Packard, Clifford Beers, in his autobiography *A Mind That Found Itself* (1908), exposed atrocious conditions of confinement. His book is an extended chronicle of how he "clamored daily for a lead pencil" from inside a mental asylum so that he could compose a petition to the governor of Connecticut as well as write his autobiography, which exposed oppressive conditions (179–80). Beers explains that he had to use covert means to sneak his letter to the governor out of the asylum. Beers's text indicates that writing inside some asylums (at a later period) by inmates was discouraged.

In addition to Packard and Beers, other important communications from disability culture during this period include "Open Letters" in *The Opal*, a newsletter published by the patients at the New York State Insane Asylum in Utica in the 1850s. Authors remained anonymous, though articles were sometimes signed with initials. In an 1852 article, an asylum inmate wrote a letter "To His Excellency Governor Hunt" (the same ex-governor who attended the opening ceremony of the asylum at Syracuse), anonymously petitioning the governor to abolish capital punishment. Through this and other open letters such as "Address to Our Patrons," inmates attempted to establish an authoritative identity in the consciousness of people outside the asylum. But the pupils inside the New York State Asylum at Syracuse were not given the type of voice that a newsletter would have provided. It would not be until the 1970s that the asylum at Syracuse would install a "patient advisory board" and the inmates at the Syracuse State School could find a voice within the walls of the institution.

Because actions are performed outside of texts, there must be a way to discover the pupil's sense of *parole*—from the French term describing what an inmate did (also meaning speech or discourse more generally). In "The Underlife of a Public Institution" (a chapter in *Asylums*), Erving Goffman discusses subversive acts that occur in an asylum. But for Goffman, the inmate is not able to talk about (or make "real" or write) what is actually happening to her; rather, the focus of discourse is on what is *supposed* to be happening to her. The asylum letters tell us something more about education as it was supposed to be than how it actually was.

Instead of asking what writings pupils left, we must ask what rhetorical action we can infer based on the inscriptions and artifacts that were left behind by the institution. Even though the pupils' speaking or writing was not preserved or advocated for, the absence of words evokes a presence. Cheryl Glenn might argue that this silence is even "a linguistic art" in itself (*Unspoken*, 160). My main conclusion to this historiographic dilemma of trying to open silences is that while there is such a thing as a history *waiting to be told*, there is also such a thing as a history that is *really hard to tell*. When I look to the letters, I see much complexity: I find a stifling amount of bureaucratic artifice woven among good intentions and motives of doing what people thought was right. As someone trying to search for alternative voices to the institutional voice, I cannot reach far outside the rhetorical accretion, selectivity, silencing, effects of display, and recurring anonymity that predominate within asylum discourse. Thus, I can name silence as *the* predominating consequence of the education at the asylum.

But silence also is accompanied by much activity. Pupils and their families participated in rhetorical practices—reading, writing, speaking, listening, responding, not responding, negotiating, resisting. Many language practices existed: as part of their education, the pupils practiced recitation of the Lord's Prayer and other dictation, they perfected their handwriting, wrote from copy, and wrote in their own words (apparently infrequently). The pupils and their families did not have the power of cultural production but they did act rhetorically. Pupils imprinted the stamp of the institution on its letterhead, they jumped over the wall to escape what they must have considered incarceration, and their families advocated for them to gain admittance, to leave the asylum, and in the case of Mrs. Thornton/Whead, to stay on through the summer as requested.

If we fail to collect remnants and thus bring presence to what is seemingly silent in the historical record of the asylum-school, we fail to do justice to historical erasures. My point in doing this work is that we do not have to *know* the exact experience in order to acknowledge its existence and power. Rather, we have to recognize that something happened—that remnants of experience exist—and that we will not necessarily be able to precisely recreate experience from the language that remains. However, if we cannot easily access the points of view and evidence we desire, we still must at least try.

CHAPTER 5

Conclusion

Idiocy—An Old, Worn-out Story

All people are subject to the same law of development.

—H. B. Wilbur

The Sheltered Workshop versus the World

The quote above, by Superintendent Wilbur, evokes the precariousness that lies at the core of all educational philosophy: *Are* all people subject to the same law of development, and if so how do we justify inequities in educational opportunity? On the other hand, if all people are *not* subject to the same law of development, how can diverse methods and flexible curricula produce equal opportunity? In the early part of the twentieth century, we saw these questions of educational justice played out in the "Great Debate" between Booker T. Washington and W. E. B. DuBois. Washington advocated for industrial education as a means for black people to gain some economic advancement; people then and now have argued that this was a "philosophy of accommodation." Conversely, DuBois argued for advancement in terms of higher education such that black communities could develop doctors, teachers, economists, lawyers, academics, leaders, politically minded people, and be represented among other professions and identities that were viewed as paths to full integration in the social and political spheres. These questions of equal opportunity and "full" integration are also central to concerns within the disability rights movement in that scholars and activists argue that industrial education, although it typically has been the touchstone of education for people with disabilities for centuries, should not necessarily be, by default, their only option.

By examining the education offered in the early years of the New York State Asylum at Syracuse, we can develop new understandings around the issue of who should be educated and how. I would argue that the education at the asylum-school centered around complex and extensive practices of becoming. In this sense, education was enveloped in the urge to improve. The education was teacher-imposed training that developed the moral (disposition, decorum, conduct, character, virtue, sensibility, volition/will), physical (comportment, delivery, speaking, listening), intellectual/mental (reading, writing, orthography, deliberation, reasoning, self-assertion, self-expression, imitation, memory, invention), and vocational aspects of a person. Education has always entailed some sort of attempted transformation, in the performance of which those who institute curricula promote what they consider to be the "common good," as measured through students' participation in social, civic, and/or political spheres.

But how much, and what kind, of participation constitutes equity? We see resistance to the inequity still at work in sheltered workshops today, where people with intellectual disabilities work in factory-like conditions for well below minimum wage. Similarly, in the context of the asylum-school, training manifests in democratic decision making in the public sphere. Wilbur's and Seguin's ideologies included perspectives on embodied difference that allowed for a limited type of education (though it was progressive for its time), but that did not mean that people gained the right to vote, were trained to profess political opinions, deliberate, or persuade in terms of their political beliefs. Rather, training consisted of bending the will toward somatic and mental normalcy, which produced a controllable and exploitable unit of labor. Pupils at the school were "taken in" and filed under the category of "unfit"; an attempt was then made through a rigorous educational and rehabilitative curriculum to make them fit for the *vita activa* (active life). Yet, the active life in the context of this institutional site meant a type of limited, civic empowerment: just enough knowledge and ability so that one could serve as domestic worker, seamstress, railroad worker, Erie Canal worker, or farmhand.

This iteration of education was a departure from the education offered at, for example, the nearby, newly chartered Syracuse University. As a counterpart to the asylum-school, in 1871 Syracuse University enrolled forty-one students in courses in algebra, geometry, Latin, Greek, history, physiology, elocution, and rhetoric.[1] Both the asylum-school and the university were strategically built atop hills that face each other in Syracuse. While the university prioritized the advancement of academic literacies, and taught elocution and rhetoric assuming that its students (the majority of whom were white men) could access public spaces with ease, the asylum-school taught rhetorical and civic education geared to transmitting moral, physiological, low-level vocational, and domestic literacies to a population that was essentially disqualified from public and civic participation beyond industrial vocation. Those educated on the more central university hill were considered to be operating within their competences;[2] students at the asylum-school on the hill near the outskirts of the city were considered a burden and public nuisance, although they would go on to gain competence in low-level domestic, industrial, and agricultural vocations.

Conventionally, rhetoric is writing and speaking in public (civic) locations, but, as this comparison between locations demonstrates, presence and participation can take on many meanings and manifest in various practices. What made the asylum-school's model of education unique was its profound attempt to transform a person's physiological, psychological, intellectual, and moral nature into "something else." And while all of education embodies these types of transformation, the asylum-school's method was especially unique because of its concern for what was considered deep-rooted mental and physical abnormality.

The Price of "Education"

As has often been the case historically for people with disabilities, these "educational" methods exacted a price. As Brueggemann, Baynton, and numerous other scholars have pointed out, educational and rehabilitative training often come at the expense of people who do not fit within normative modes of communication or bodily expression. One way this price is paid is through painful physiological rehabilitative mechanisms (strategies akin to what we think of as physical therapy). However, the price exacted in the asylum-school is difficult to know because of the gaps and silences in the historical record; nonetheless, when practices in the asylum are situated in relationship to other practices—for example, alongside the broader genre of disability epistolary (as I have done in chapter 4) or alongside the education offered at Syracuse University during the same time period—we can imagine that some sort of price was exacted by the rigor of a segregated education that aimed to perform a complete overhaul, wherein pupils' freedom of movement was restricted and more often than not their participation was involuntary. Certainly the physical contraptions that were utilized in the gymnasium, which I describe in chapter 3, offer an example of a price some may have paid for normalcy.

That is not to say that there were heroes and villains. While the schooling they propounded was far from perfect, I acknowledge that Dr.

Seguin and Superintendent Wilbur created a systematic curriculum that, first and foremost, worked to promote the student's entry into a social life of relation whereby the student could engage in "ordinary" endeavors and enter into the "common life." I recognize that education (including vocational) is not necessarily neutral, liberatory, nor wholly oppressive. However, while vocational participation was foregrounded in the asylum-school over participation in public deliberation or the political use of language, pupils were able to expand their life options, regardless of how limited those options may have been. As hard as it was for me to let go of the notion, I am forced to acknowledge that Wilbur and Seguin—the good doctors—could not have been villains, and the Thorntons, the other families, and their children, the pupils, could not have been heroes. Wilbur *believed* that his pupils could learn, and this notion certainly was not a dominant view during his time. Yet, despite Wilbur's progressive thinking, the institutional voice dominates the historical record at the expense of other "voices," as I have demonstrated in my search for traces—remnants—of Mrs. Thornton and her son, Jimmy.

Inscribing Presence

My search was encumbered by much more than simply the predominance of dominant perspectives. Related obstacles included issues of rhetorical accretion (layering of discourse), the literate disconnection (inability to read and write) of pupils, lack of self-historicization, and the lack of archival evidence regarding nondominant groups. While one motto of the disability rights movement is *nothing about us without us*, my research has confronted specific evidentiary challenges that make it nearly impossible to represent some people through their own words. One of the questions that pervades the field of disability history has been, "What are the lived experiences of people with disabilities, in their own words?" But, for example, if one examines the well-known life of the Wild Boy of Averyron—a speechless boy who was found in the woods in France in 1799 and was then taught by Jean Marc Gaspard Itard (Seguin's teacher), one of the first special educators—one finds that the boy literally had no words of his own, no text of his own experience from his own perspective. His life is known only through Itard's account of it. So, then, how is his presence created?

Likewise, the lives of most of the people who lived at the asylum-school can be reconstructed only through secondary or tertiary sources—layers of rhetorical accretion (Vicki Collins) that mediate language farther away from its source. Without direct access to the words or sentiments of the students/inmates themselves, I derive experiences from second- and third-person accounts found in medical files, newspaper and journal articles, curriculum and archival documents. These disparate and idiosyncratic sources together constitute a rhetoric of remnants that does not profess truth but rather offers multiple possibilities in order to foreground presence over absence. In these documents, the student/patient is first and foremost constructed as an object of medical and rehabilitative intervention, rather than as a decision-making, credible, and vital person with a life outside of medical and rehabilitative necessity. A rhetoric of remnants attempts to inscribe subjectivity.

There are scholars who have in fact begun to sort through the layers of mediation that occur in medicalized rhetoric. Both Susan Wells, in *Out of the Dead House,* and Michael Rembis, in "'I Ain't Had Much Schooling': The Ritual of Examination and the Social Construction of Impairment," analyze "voice" through rhetorical accretion. Study of the layering of perspective is an effective tool for historical analysis; the challenge is to disentangle the layers of mediation in order to reveal not only how "original" sentiments are manipulated but also what those sentiments may have been in the first place.

Nevertheless, while Wells and Rembis have much primary text to analyze, the words or personal sentiments of students/inmates at the asylum-school are largely unavailable. There are no significant writings from which to draw; only tiny remnants exist of their own inscriptions. This lack of primary, autobiographical writing or significant writing of any kind is not a unique occurrence confined to the lives of only a few people with disabilities. Rather, Biklen and Kliewer argue that large societal biases against intellectual capacity have been, and still remain, a justification for the imposition of subliteracy. They contend that access to citizenship in literate communities is difficult (and was difficult in the past) for most people with intellectual disabilities because society presumes an inherent stasis in them; that is, they are thought to be beyond the reach of literacy and even beyond the potential for education. Biklen and Kliewer go on to say that even when people with disabilities do gain access to written literacy, they are constructed as "parrots" or their acts of writing are believed not to have come from them. This imposition of subliteracy offers another angle to the problem of historical erasure.

Presence, thus, takes on a different flavor—I had to consider that which was unspoken. Take, for example, case no. 245 from *Pupil Evaluation Reports* of 1870 (B1666 [ca. 1860–1909]). J. B. arrived at the asylum in Syracuse in 1870 at the age of sixteen, from New Paltz County House. When brought to the asylum-school he was sick, but the report goes on to say that, as soon as he was able to walk again, he fled from the asylum. This is certainly, as Glenn would agree, a "silent rhetorical display" (20). These instances of resistance through running away, or what the institution called "elopement," are seen consistently throughout the records in the annual reports and other institutional documents.

The notations of these elopements are inscriptions or writings that fix the rhetorical actions of the pupils in history. The "inscription of action" (Geertz, 31) transforms their silence into a linguistic structure (a presence or remnant) in the historical record. Clifford Geertz discusses the extent to which inscription of action can "persist in a way its actuality cannot" (*Local Knowledge*, 31). In the cultural location of the asylum-school, inscription of action happened regardless of who was speaking or writing. We can extract a more complete picture of what occurred, then, from an action that was inscribed only partially.

That being said, while work in the print shop, in the sewing room, in the field, or in the army may not have engaged with literacy directly, it constituted an unspoken and unwritten form of communicative (i.e., rhetorical) action. When Glenn writes that "a person cannot not communicate," she illustrates the rationale behind my attempt to historicize silence in the asylum-school (16). The social history of this location must be told through actions rather than texts and words. Actions are never muted; rather, they give presence. We have to recognize that something happened, however silently, and that we will not necessarily be able to always recreate it from language. Silence can generate meaning, and that meaning can illuminate rhetorical action in a way that includes things other than speaking and writing.

The remnants from the asylum-school are important because if we memorialize only that which is fully preserved in written form, we run the risk of keeping the margins of history *on* the margins of history. This work embodies an impetus to (re)consider who the subjects of history are and where we locate our studies. This book seeks to relocate practices and experiences that were previously considered marginal into the center, compelling us to rethink terminology and conceptual anchors. I use the past as a way to invigorate how I conceptualize persuasion, participation, citizenship, becoming, and communication. The field of rhetoric has already committed to looking for meaning in new places and spaces, and I do social history here in order to displace the notion that only certain types of people are worthy of study. Rather, education has various context and site-dependent manifestations, all of which can be equally valid and relevant to people working in various areas of education and advocacy.

Straightening Up and Straightening Out

Still, we need to better understand how norms emerge through rhetoric and education. How do ideologies *persuade* us that physiological perfection is the "reality" for which we all should strive? The arts of becoming have been constituted by stringent imperatives to straighten out physically, straighten up behaviorally, speak correctly, and walk evenly (Cicero, Quintilian, Sheridan, etc.), but also by the notion that without this transformation—this rehabilitation—eloquence, and civic, intellectual, and rhetorical fitness may never be achieved. In this sense, normalization is an important and problematic organizing principle; physiognomics, or the conflation between virtuosity/eloquence and adherence to bodily norms, is very present still in our educational endeavors and in our rhetoric. While these imperatives ordinarily share a causal relationship—for example, a certain aesthetic, tone of voice, or way of moving the body brings about eloquence—it is important to look to diverse sites such as the asylum-school to attempt to disrupt the naturalization of these norms. As the familiar narrative goes, with enough training, physical grace, or beauty, one can become relatively refined, reformed, and successful. The will toward rectitude is left unquestioned because our ideology is ensconced in pursuits of perfection. Education has always formed an interested rather than neutral foundation for the valuation of imperatives related to character, aesthetics, eloquence, skill, achievement, training, and transformation. These imperatives are cultural practices, and educational practice has characteristically measured and discursively produced exclusionary norms with regard to them.

In this sense, rhetoric includes ways in which Wilbur and Seguin transformed their vision of the norm into pedagogy. David Gold calls attention to "the value of diverse, institutional microhistories that assume a fluid relationship between ideology and pedagogy" (Gold, 2). The site of the asylum-school offers a useful model for ways in which pedagogy as discourse and action can fashion or impose a particularly normalized, and often limited or nominal, way of being in the world. From this study of the asylum-school, we can see how a particular population received a different (arguably unequal) type of education.

Further consideration is necessary of the effect that normalization and medicalization have had on education. It will be important in the future to understand more about how pathologies of the body and mind have constructed essentialized ways of thinking. For example, Brad Byrom, Douglas Baynton, and numerous others working in disability studies see the end of the nineteenth century as a monumental period—the rise of medical science and the scientific determination of disability or "handicap." This shift to medical authority involved private organizations as well as large institutions taking control away from immediate communities. Societies transitioned from religious to medical authority; yet this enormous cultural shift has been mostly undertheorized. The field of disability studies shows that rehabilitation and medical authority are transformative social events that have been historically enmeshed in complicated and important rhetorics. Moreover, key institutions and what Snyder and Mitchell call "cultural locations of disability" merit attention from scholars—locations such as hospitals, sheltered workshops, asylums, and homes for the aged. My book nudges conversations forward concerning the effect of medicalization and other deficit models. But perhaps most importantly, in order to do this work, as Brueggemann, Fredal, and Dolmage urge us, we must dispel the notion that disability or deformity precludes achievement. Further, disability must gain a positive signification so that we stop reading history normatively.

In the project, I reconceive of education broadly as an education that has rhetorical and ideological aspects to it that coalesce around technologies of normalization. Certainly, all pedagogy or education is rhetorical and ideological in the ways it is deployed. But this site shows us further how rhetoric is also not only the negotiation that we engage in with each other (privately and civically, individually and collectively, and silently and discursively) to attempt to reconcile our multiplicitous understandings of "truth" and "reality," but it is also the negotiation we engage in as we attempt to approximate and challenge and resist norms related to communication, physical embodiment, and intellectual capacity. Rhetoric creates and recreates norms. Education—and even more so, *we*—impose those norms.

Strength in Variation

In order to counter the problem of exclusionary imperatives, we can consider how the notion or metaphor of the "speechless idiot" (the "half-wit") operates as an implicit and often unrecognized antithesis to success—the skilled intellectual, speaker, writer, academic, and orator. My work suggests that the construction of "idiocy" operates as a nemesis to "the great orator": without the figure of the speechless "idiot," the figure of the eloquent orator does not have the same worth. Additionally, without the asylum on the outskirts of town, Syracuse University could not, perhaps, have such elevated stature in our minds. Rather than viewing embodied difference as a biological essence, my research suggests that we conceive of intellectual competence and intellectual difference as socially and rhetorically constructed. In essence, my work aims to bring us closer to understanding complexities of the human condition: difference, vulnerability (at times), and strength (at times) in variation. "Idiocy" is an ideology, a social construction, and most importantly, a rhetorical and educational commonplace that warrants critique. We must become more conscious of the ways we construct educational spaces as the antithesis of other spaces and how we construct "idiocy" as the foil to success.

Our challenge is to move beyond the notion of disability as deficit to arrive at people's social historicity as agents even when they do not speak or write. The limitations and the successes in the asylum-school's curriculum point to challenges in terms of how we dare to create spaces for education that move beyond production, vocation, established norms, and postindustrial anonymity. By this, I mean to emphasize that teaching embodies civic participation in the form of social responsibility, decision making, problem solving, invention, and relationship. When we recover diverse sites, we can ask ourselves to reevaluate our own educational intentions, exclusions, and ways in which we prepare (or fail to prepare) students for civic life. This study shows how education theoretically and in practice subjects all people to similar laws of development that emphasize movement of the will, connecting sensations to ideas, transforming a "reflex" (Dr. Seguin's term) or robotic life into a self-regulating life, and usefulness in civic endeavors. Because variability is universal, we can come to value its manifestation in students, histories, and pedagogies. We too often rely heavily upon an assumed sameness of the human condition. Rather, education can also be interested in variability of the human condition. In essence, all education is "special," and "idiocy" is an old, worn-out story of the past. Yet it is also quite the persistent metaphor.

Notes

Front Matter/Dedication

See the Self-Advocates of Central New York at http://thechp.syr.edu/sacny.htm.

Chapter 1. Introduction

1. To read more on actions related to the gap problems, see htttp://disabledinaction.org. Also see "Mind the Gap," *New York Times*, August 20, 2006. This article reports that in 2004, there were fifty-nine platform gap accidents.

2. Throughout, I use the term *idiot* with and without quotation marks. In both instances, it should be understood as a socially constructed, medicalized term in use in the mid-nineteenth century.

3. The term *feeble-minded* came into common use in the 1870s to partially replace *idiot*. It wasn't until the start of the twentieth century that the labels subdivided into moron, idiot, and imbecile. Today, we would equate these labels to those of intellectual disability, mental retardation (which is going out of use), and developmental disability. However, standards for determinations were very different then which means that many people who would not be labeled as having a disability today would have been labeled that way during the time of my study and vice versa. Discrimination based on race, class, and gender played a large part in determinations during the time period and, some say, still do today. Few, if any, nonwhite or newly immigrated pupils were accepted into the asylum from 1853–1883, and race and disability were entangled such that disability and deviance were exceedingly read onto nonwhite, nonimmigrant bodies.

4. In 1878, Binet was a researcher at Salpetrière Hospital in Paris, the same hospital where Dr. Seguin began teaching in 1841. Binet was assigned to set up a

test that measured the difference between an "ordinary" child and a child seemingly wanting in mental faculties. In 1903, he published *Experimental Studies of Intelligence*, which describes thirty tasks given to a child to determine their mental age and thus educational placement. Binet affirmed that his test had limitations such as negating variability of the development of children. Regardless, Henry Goddard altered Binet's test in the United States by using it to falsely demonstrate superiority of white, able-bodied people.

5. Marcus Tullius Cicero (106–43 BCE), the famous Roman philosopher, orator, and political theorist believed that oratory, when used correctly, benefited individuals and the state. Oratory was understood to unite speakers and audiences in a shared vision.

6. One narrative of Demosthenes says that in order to succeed as an orator he first had to eliminate his stutter through rigorous training. However, Martha Rose in *The Staff of Oedipus: Transforming Disability in Ancient Greece* poses a different narrative in arguing that disability in Ancient Greece was not always viewed as a misfortune that had to be overcome in order to succeed and, further, that there is no definitive evidence that proves that Demosthenes was indeed a stutterer (50–57).

7. Throughout the book, I rely heavily upon Cheryl Glenn's work in *Unspoken: A Rhetoric of Silence* (Carbondale: Southern Illinois University Press, 2004).

8. This gravestone resides at the Center on Human Policy and Disability Studies at Syracuse University.

9. The annual reports were largely written by Superintendent Wilbur with an introduction by the board of trustees. They were addressed to the Legislature of the State of New York in Albany. Wilbur lays out much of the curriculum in these reports.

10. See Jay Dolmage, "Disabled Upon Arrival. The Rhetorical Construction of Disability and Race at Ellis Island," *Cultural Critique* 77 (Winter 2011): 24–69.

11. Howe was husband of the women's rights advocate Julia Ward Howe and founder of the famous Perkins Institute for the Blind where Helen Keller was educated. Howe was also an abolitionist, fighter for the Greek Revolution, and advocate for women's rights. Mann, Howe, and Superintendent Wilbur traveled in the same professional circles; Horace Mann visited and attested to the success of the Syracuse asylum.

12. Those who showed support for the asylum-school included the Legislature of New York; Allen Monroe, mayor of Syracuse; Elias W. Leavenworth, New York's secretary of state and president of Syracuse Savings Institution, the Water Works Company, and the Gas Light Company; the Honorable Washington Hunt, ex-governor; the current governor, Horatio Seymour.

13. An uncomfortable giggle has been a frequent response when I share the name of my site of study (The New York State Asylum for Idiots).

14. The contemporary politically correct term would be *inclusive education*. Whatever the name, the practices are still segregated. I use "special" here to signify that the domain of rhetorical education for people with disabilities warrants recognition.

15. A spin on Erving Goffman's "The Underlife of an Institution," from his *Asylums: Essays on the Social Situation of Mental Patients and Other Inmates* (New York: Doubleday, 1961).

Chapter 2. "Confusion into Order Changed"

1. Chapter 4 chronicles deaf education more specifically.

2. Seguin's work descended from Pinel, Itard, and Pestalozzi and extended forward to Montessori and Dewey. More discussion of specific educational methods can be found in chapter 3.

3. For further explanation of epideictic rhetoric, see "Epideictic Rhetoric and the Reinvention of Disability: A Study of Ceremony at the New York State Asylum for 'Idiots'" by Zosha Stuckey. This article uses epideictic rhetoric to examine how the intellectually disabled person was, over time, constructed *and* deconstructed via praise and blame. http://www.presenttensejournal.org/category/volume-2/issue-2/.

4. Uttered at the opening ceremony by the ex-secretary of state, Hon. Christopher Morgan. 4th *Annual Report*, 211.

5. See Louis C. Charland, "Benevolent Theory: Moral Treatment at the York Retreat," *History of Psychiatry* 18, no. 1(2007): 61–80.

6. Howe was the husband of the women's rights advocate Julia Ward Howe.

7. May, a Unitarian minister, founder of the normal school system, abolitionist, and part organizer of the Jerry Rescue in 1851 in Syracuse, was instrumental in establishing the public school system in Syracuse at mid-century.

8. See discussion in the following paragraph of the Individuals with Disabilities Education Act of 1974.

9. Mental capacity continued to be assessed after Wilbur's time. Dolmage explains how inspections created "heterotopias of deviance" at Ellis Island in the early twentieth century and were "cursory" and "largely a matter of intuition, a kind of magical medical view" thought to access the "intuitive ability" of the inspector ("Disabled," 34, 45); Ellis Island shaped the culture's capacity for body reading at a glance in everyone (45). Dolmage calls this a "snapshot diagnosis" (36).

10. I use the word *unique* not to ignore the enumerative strategies that bring about anonymity in prisons and other institutions but rather because I wish to draw attention to how anonymity could function.

11. Interestingly, "Nattie and Willie" appear more than once in the archives.

12. African Americans, according to Dix, were immune to insanity because she believed that insanity affected only those who, due to industrialization, had lost their connection to cultured living and black people to her were not cultured. Despite her racist beliefs, Dix was an avid witness to abuses that occurred in poorhouses, though she did not advocate for any African Americans she encountered.

13. Further discussion along these lines continues in chapter 4.

Chapter 3. In Pursuit of the Active Life

1. I will discuss in detail each of these terms as I come upon them in this chapter.

2. In terms of contemporary discourse, the phrase *special education* is outdated. The contemporary, politically correct term would be "inclusive education," because it points to the attempt to merge special with general education. Whatever the name, the practices are still more often segregated. I use "special" here to

signify that the domain of education for people with disabilities is bifurcated from "general" education. Both "special" and "inclusive" are anachronistic with regard to the mid-nineteenth century.

3. Reverend Samuel J. May was a prominent abolitionist and progressive educational reformer in Syracuse.

4. Winzer locates the "first authentic special education efforts" in the sixteenth century, when hereditary deafness prominent in Spain's royalty inspired laws of inheritance that stipulated that males had to be able to speak to inherit; thus, deaf males from wealthy families received lessons in orality (31–32). While Winzer offers a detailed history of "special education," I focus my history on "special" education of those labeled as "idiots" in the nineteenth century. See Winzor, McDonough, and Trent for a more comprehensive discussion. As with any history, the exact "start" of something is contested. I do claim that the asylum-school was the start of systematized, public education for "idiots" in the United States.

5. The "oral method" of teaching those who were deaf to speak verbally has been, and still is, highly contested. To read more on this, see Douglas Baynton, *Forbidden Signs: American Culture and the Campaign Against Sign Language* (Chicago: University of Chicago Press, 1996, Brenda Brueggemann, *Lend Me Your Ear: Rhetorical Constructions of Deafness* (Washington, DC: Gallaudet University Press, 1999, Padden and Humphries, *Inside Deaf Culture* (Cambridge: Harvard University Press, 2005)., and R. A. R. Edwards, *Words Made Flesh: Nineteenth Century Deaf Education and the Growth of Deaf Culture* (New York: New York University Press, 2012). Edwards points to the "oralist" movement, which was popular in England and Germany during this time, while France focused more on sign language, manual alphabet, and mechanical signs (the language grammatically signed). In the United States, Gallaudent and Clerc were largely against teaching deaf students to speak while S. G. Howe, A. G. Bell, and H. Mann were in favor of it. In 1900, the oral method was primary in 40 percent of deaf schools; by 1920, oralism was primary in 80 percent of the schools (Padden, 48).

6. I have not found any indication that sign language was used, though it is unlikely that deaf pupils would have entirely abandoned their "home signs." In *Words Made Flesh*, Edwards presents a thorough history of American Sign Language as having emerged gradually in residential schools from the "idiosyncratic natural signs" that pupils used at home, with each other, and with their teachers (44–45). It is likely that bilingual-bicultural education for deaf pupils (ASL being primary and English acting as the second language) was not the case at the asylum-school.

7. While this statement presumes that oralism for deaf students was not the primary method at the asylum-school, there are other instances in the archive where it appears that it was (see the following paragraph). I can only reconcile these inconsistencies by pointing out the fluidity of curriculum and noting that "language" must have often been conflated with "speech."

8. This way of imposing the will onto the student is similar to the pedagogical use of the will discussed by Isocrates in *Antidosis*.

9. See Elof Carlson, *The Unfit: The History of a Bad Idea* (Cold Spring Harbor, NY: Cold Spring Harbor Press, 2001; and Nancy Ordover, *American Eugenics: Race, Queer Anatomy, and the Science of Nationalism* (Minneapolis: University of Minnesota Press, 2003).

10. The State Board of Charities in New York was run by Josephine Shaw Lowell, who also was the main proponent of the new custodial asylum for girls in Newark, New York. Lowell was the sister of Robert Gould Shaw, known for his command of the all-black 54th regiment in the Civil War. The Newark Custodial Asylum for Feeble-minded Women of Childbearing Age deserves a lengthy discussion that I do not have space for here. See Nicole Rafter, *Creating Born Criminals* (Urbana: University of Illinois Press, 1997).

11. See my discussion of a revised understanding of the term *civic* on pages 2–3 where civic connotes more than oratorical or political presence.

Chapter 4. In Pursuit of the Underlife of the Archive

The chapter title is intended as a spin on Erving Goffman's "The Underlife of an Institution," a chapter from *Asylums*.

1. I do not mean a physiological sense of listening but rather I use the word *listen* to mean holding attention.

2. Because these are the only examples of writing by pupils themselves, I have extended my time period for these two artifacts.

3. Another paradox of rhetorical history is how the discourse and, in this instance sentiment, is always going to be interpreted through my comparative lens even though I do my best to try and understand the particular historical context of the period.

4. Throughout the chapter, I rely heavily upon Cheryl Glenn's work in *Unspoken: A Rhetoric of Silence*.

5. This notion that silence does not necessarily signify absence is from the work of Cheryl Glenn in *Unspoken: A Rhetoric of Silence*. I extend Glenn's notion of silence to look at the cultural significance especially for Deafness, American Sign Language, and disability. In disability studies, the silence of Deafness and disability is not a pathology nor is it always "tactical"; rather, silence is an altogether different way of life when one's reality doesn't include sound or speaking. For my purposes, silence *is* productive, as Glenn argues, when it creates opportunities to conceptualize historical narratives from subaltern perspectives.

6. Jacqueline Jones Royster's concept in which she "reconstruct[s] historical pathways" by reading "between the lines and around the 'facts' and artifacts" (81–82).

7. Lore and gossip mention a fire that burned many of the asylum records, but this cannot be confirmed, which is why it and many other scenarios remain mere possibilities.

8. Each of the three sets of letters in this chapter was found in a separate archive (see works cited). However, all of the letters have received institutional approval and therefore represent an institutionally sanctioned narrative. Further on in the chapter, I discuss more of the context for my discovery of the letters.

9. Poster's work on epistolary is focused on Greco-Roman Antiquity; Lipson, as I mention, writes on Ancient Egyptian rhetoric.

10. I have seen both "Whead" and "Wheat" as spellings of her name after remarriage.

11. For a detailed history of the development of Sign Language in residential schools in the nineteenth century, see Edwards and Padden. Both authors explain how deaf pupils came to residential schools with a "natural language of signs" which was their own form of signing employed at home and with others (Edwards, 35–36). While American Sign Language developed over time from an amalgamation of various sign dialects, by 1855 Howe and Mann had bolstered a movement against Sign that advocated Oralism (articulation and speech). The asylum-school in my study appears to have utilized a combination of Sign and Oralism while Jimmy was a pupil there. See chapter 3.

12. I infer that he was a state-funded pupil rather than a privately paying one for many reasons: if he had been a privately paying pupil, he most likely would not have arrived anonymously at the asylum, he most likely would have already had all of his clothes provided for him, most likely his mother would not have had the asylum pay for his return trip home in 1862, and most likely we would have documentation of Christmas and other gifts sent to him.

13. At the time Jimmy attended the asylum-school, "ordinary" children ("ordinary" was used then as we use "normal" or "non-disabled" today) of Syracuse were receiving free "universal" education. It is not likely, however, that Jimmy's teachers in Cincinnatus would have known sign language even if Jimmy had attended school there. Therefore, his acceptance into the asylum-school would arguably have been his only opportunity to receive an adequate education.

14. We see this again in Letter Seven which I discuss farther along in the chapter, as H. H. Saville tells Mrs. Thornton that Jimmy is better off at the asylum-school than he would be at home.

15. I can easily deduce the approximate date and sequencing of the letter based on its content.

16. The letter writer, Mulford, was the asylum's matron from its beginning in 1852 until 1871. Mulford would have been second in command directly under Wilbur. She would have had under her management all of the teachers (who were female), the assistants (who dressed, washed, and performed the more menial tasks with the pupils), and the "servants" or housekeepers and kitchen workers. The "steward" was the male equivalent of the matron (Mr. Saville, the letter writer of Letters Seven and Eight, might have been the steward); the steward managed the functions of the asylum considered within the province of male labor such as farming, grading and landscaping, and maintenance and repair.

17. The letter writers who were not family members included people who wrote for parents who may not have had knowledge of written English, or people who served as pupils' legal guardians.

18. Most likely, the institution's seal was made and used in the asylum's print shop where, beginning in the 1880s, inmates worked.

19. To learn more about literacy and people with developmental disabilities, one can look to the work of the Self-Advocacy Movement, as represented in books such as *New Voices: Self-Advocacy by People with Disabilities*, ed. by Dybwad and Bersani, 1996. Aims of this movement include increased access to literacy for people previously considered incapable of competence in that area. See also Margaret Winzer, *The History of Special Education: From Isolation to Integration* (Washington,

DC: Gallaudet University Press, 1993); and Douglas Biklen and Christopher Kliewer, "Who May Be Literate?: Disability and Resistance to the Cultural Denial of Competence," *American Educational Research Journal* 43, no. 2 (Summer 2006): 163–92.

Chapter 5. "Idiocy": An Old, Worn-Out Story

1. http://archives.syr.edu/history/.

2. In *Liberating Language: Sites of Rhetorical Education in Nineteenth-Century Black America*, Shirley Wilson Logan uses the terms *rhetorical competence* and *rhetorical acumen* (6, 9) to discuss how an education in rhetoric can allow people to engage in self-improvement and self-empowerment in the face of oppressive social structures.

Bibliography

Agnew, Lois. *Outward, Visible Propriety*. Columbia: University of South Carolina Press, 2008.

Annual Proceedings of the Steuben County Board of Supervisors, 1891 and 1895.

Annual Reports of the New York State Asylum for Idiots, 1852–1884, transmitted to the Legislature New York State Asylum for Idiots. Obtained in part from http://www. disabilityhistorymuseum.org, Stephen J. Taylor personal collection, and the Museum at the Developmental Disabilities Service Office, Syracuse.

Aristotle. *On Rhetoric: A Theory of Civic Discourse*. Edited by George Kennedy. New York: Oxford University Press, 1991, 2007.

Atwood, Margaret. *Der blinde Mörder* (*The Blind Assassin*). New York: Bloomsbury, 2000.

Baynton, Douglas. "Disability and the Justification of Inequality in American History." In *The New Disability History: American Perspectives*, edited by Longmore and Umansky. New York: New York University Press, 2001.

———. *Forbidden Signs: American Culture and the Campaign Against Sign Language*. Chicago: University of Chicago Press, 1996.

Beers, Clifford. *A Mind That Found Itself*. Garden City: Doubleday, 1908.

Berkenkotter, Carol. *Patient Tales: Case Histories and the Uses of Narrative in Psychiatry*. Columbia: University of South Carolina Press, 2008.

Berlin, James. "Revisionary Histories of Rhetoric: Politics, Power, and Plurality." In *Writing Histories of Rhetoric*, edited by V. Vitanza. Carbondale: Southern Illinois University Press, 1994.

Berube, Michael. *Life as We Know It: A Father, A Family, and an Exceptional Child*. New York: Vintage, 1998.

Biklen, Douglas, and Christopher Kliewer. "Who May Be Literate?: Disability and Resistance to the Cultural Denial of Competence." *American Educational Research Journal* 43, no. 2 (Summer 2006): 163–92.

Bogdan, Robert. *Freak Show*. Chicago: University of Chicago Press, 1988.

———. Personal Interview. April 15, 2010.

———, and Steven J. Taylor. "Relationships with Severely Disabled People: The Social Construction of Humanness." *Social Problems* 36, no. 2 (April 1989): 135–48.

Brueggemann, Brenda. *Deaf Subjects: Between Identities and Places*. New York: New York University Press, 2009.

———. *Lend Me Your Ear: Rhetorical Constructions of Deafness*. Washington, DC: Gallaudet University Press, 1999.

Buchanan, Lindal. *Regendering Delivery: The Fifth Canon and Antebellum Women Rhetors*. Carbondale: Southern Illinois University Press, 2005.

Burch, Susan. *Unspeakable: The Story of Junius Wilson*. Chapel Hill: University of North Carolina Press, 2007.

———, and Ian Sutherland. "Who's Not Yet Here: American Disability History." *Radical History Review* (Winter 2006): 127–47.

Byrom, Brad. "A Pupil and a Patient: Hospital Schools in Progressive America." In *The New Disability History: American Perspectives*, edited by Longmore and Umansky. New York: New York University Press, 2001.

Campbell, George. *Philosophy of Rhetoric*. Carbondale: Southern Illinois University Press, 1963 (1850).

Campbell, Karlyn Kohrs. "Consciousness-Raising: Linking Theory, Critics, and Practice." *RSQ* 32, no. 1 (Winter 2002).

Carey, Allison. *On The Margins of Citizenship: Intellectual Disability and Civil Rights in Twentieth-Century America*. Philadelphia: Temple University Press, 2009.

Carlson, Elof Axel. *The Unfit: The History of a Bad Idea*. Cold Spring Harbor, NY: Cold Spring Harbor Press, 2001.

Carr, Jean Ferguson, Stephen L. Carr, and Lucille M. Schultz. *Archives of Instruction: Nineteenth-Century Rhetorics, Readers, and Composition Books in the U.S.* Carbondale: Southern Illinois University Press, 2005.

Census Records, 1865, 1870, 1880. Caton, Steuben County, New York.

Census Reports. New York State Archives, Albany Cultural Education Department. B1656-99 Clipping Files to 1911.

Center on Human Policy. "As One Door Closes, Many Open." In *I Can See No Downside to the Closure of the DSO: A Documentary History of the Closure of SDC*, compiled by Hall, Mair, Harris, and Lewin. Syracuse: Center on Human Policy Press, 1999.

Charland, Louis C. "Benevolent Theory: Moral Treatment at the York Retreat." *History of Psychiatry* 18, no. 1 (2007): 61–80.

Cicero, Marcus Tullius. *De officiis*. Translated by Walter Miller. Loeb Classical Library Series. London: William Heinemann, 1913.

———. *De oratore*. Translated by J. S. Watson. Carbondale: Southern Illinois University Press, 1970.

Ciota, Bob. "Comments. As One Door Closes, Many Open." Compiled by Hall, Mair, Harris, and Lewin. Syracuse: Center on Human Policy Press, 1999.

Clark, Gregory, and Michael Halloran. "Introduction." In *Oratorical Culture in Nineteenth-Century America: Transformations in the Theory and Practice of Rhetoric*. Carbondale: Southern Illinois University Press, 1993.

Clark, Suzanne. *Sentimental Modernism: Women Writers and the Revolution of the Word*. Bloomington: Indiana University Press, 1991.

Cobb, Amanda. *Listening to Our Grandmother's Stories: Bloomfield Academy for Chickasaw Females 1852–1949, 1998*. Lincoln: University of Nebraska Press, 2000.

Collins (Tolar Burton), Vicki. "The Speaker Respoken: Material Rhetoric as Feminist Methodology." *College English* 61, no. 5 (1999): 545–73.

Condillac, Etienne. *Treatise on the Sensations*. Translated and introduced by Geraldine Carr. Los Angeles: University of Southern California Press, 1983.

Corbett, Edward. "John Locke's Contributions to Rhetoric." *College Composition and Communication* 32, no. 4 (December 1981): 423–33.

Couser, Thomas. "Signifying Bodies: Life Writing and Disability Studies." In *Disability Studies: Enabling the Humanities*, edited by Brenda Jo Brueggemann, R. Garland-Thomson, and S. Snyder. New York: Modern Language Association, 2002.

Crowley, Sharon. *The Methodical Memory*. Carbondale: Southern Illinois University Press, 1990.

Darby, Penney, and Peter Stastny. *The Lives They Left Behind: Suitcases from a State Hospital*. New York: Bellevue Literary Press, 2008.

de Certeau, Michel. *The Writing of History*. New York: Columbia University Press, 1988 (1975).

Derrida, Jacques. *Archive Fever: A Freudian Impression*. Translated by Eric Prenowitz. Chicago: University of Chicago Press, 1996.

Descriptive Register of Pupils, 1875–1879. New York State Archives, Albany Cultural Education Department.

Dewey, John. "The Future of Liberalism." In *The Later Works*, 17 vols., edited by JoAnn Boydston. Carbondale: Southern Illinois University Press, 1981–1990 (1935).

Dix, Dorothea. "Memorial to the Honorable, the Senate and House of Representatives of the State of Illinois." In *Asylum, Prison, Poorhouse: The Writings and Reform Work of Dorothea Dix in Illinois*. Carbondale: Southern Illinois University Press, 1999 (1847).

Dolmage, Jay. "Breathe Upon Us an Even Flame: Hephaestus, History, and the Body of Rhetoric." *Rhetoric Review* 25, no. 2 (2006): 119–40.

———. "Disabled upon Arrival. The Rhetorical Construction of Disability and Race at Ellis Island." *Cultural Critique* 77 (Winter 2011): 24–69.

Donawerth, Jane. *Conversational Rhetoric: The Rise and Fall of a Women's Tradition, 1600–1900*. Carbondale: Southern Illinois University Press, 2011.

Duffy, John, with Rebecca Dorner. "The Pathos of 'Mindblindness': Autism, Science, and Sadness in 'Theory of Mind' Narratives." *Journal of Literary and Cultural Disability Studies* 5, no. 2 (2011): 201–15.

———. *Writing From These Roots: The Historical Development of Literacy in a Hmong American Community*. Honolulu: University of Hawai'i Press, 2007.

Dunn, Patricia Ann. *Learning Re-Abled: The Learning Disability Controversy and Composition Studies*. Portsmouth, NH: Boynton/Cook, 1995.

———. *Talking, Sketching, Moving: Multiple Literacies in the Teaching of Writing*. Portsmouth, NH: Boynton /Cook, 2001.

Edwards, R. A. R. *Words Made Flesh: Nineteenth Century Deaf Education and the Growth of Deaf Culture*. New York: New York University Press, 2012.

Einhorn, Lois J. *Helen Keller, Public Speaker: Sightless but Seen, Deaf but Heard.* Westport, CT: Greenwood, 1998.

Enoch, Jessica. *Refiguring Rhetorical Education: Women Teaching African American, Native American, and Chicano/a Students, 1865–1911.* Carbondale: Southern Illinois University Press, 2008.

Ervelles, Nirmala. *Disability and Difference in Global Contexts: Enabling a Transformative Body.* Hampshire, UK: Palgrave Macmillan, 2011.

Exhibit material from the Pan American Exposition, 1893. New York State Archives, Albany. Cultural Education Department. B1697-00.

Fahnestock, Jeanne. *Rhetorical Figures in Science.* New York: Oxford University Press, 1999.

Ferguson, Philip. "The Doubting Dance: Contributions to a History of Parent/ Professional Interactions in Early 20th Century America." *Research & Practice for Persons with Severe Disabilities* 33, no. 1–2 (2009): 48–58.

Fletcher-Janzen, Elaine, and Cecil R. Reynolds. Concise Encyclopedia of Special Education: A Reference for the Education of the Handicapped and Other Exceptional Children and Adults. New York: Wiley and Sons, 2000.

Foucault, Michel. *The Birth of the Clinic: An Archaeology of Medical Perception.* New York: Vintage Books, 1994 (1963).

———. *Discipline and Punishment: The Birth of the Prison.* Translated by Alan M. Sheridan-Smith. New York: Vintage Books, 1979.

———. *Madness and Civilization: A History of Insanity in the Age of Reason.* New York: Routledge, 1961.

Fredal, James. *Rhetorical Action in Ancient Athens: Persuasive Artistry from Solon to Demosthenes.* Carbondale: Southern Illinois University Press, 2006.

Garland-Thomson, Rosemarie. *Extraordinary Bodies.* New York: Columbia University Press, 1997.

Geertz, Clifford. *Local Knowledge: Further Essays in Interpretive Anthropology.* New York: Basic Books, 1983.

Gere, Anne Ruggles. *Intimate Practices: Literacy and Cultural Work in U.S. Women's Clubs 1880–1920.* Champaign: University of Illinois Press, 1997.

Glenn, Cheryl. "Introduction." In *Rhetorical Education in America.* Tuscaloosa: University of Alabama Press, 2009.

———. *Unspoken: A Rhetoric of Silence.* Carbondale: Southern Illinois University Press, 2004.

Goddard, Henry. *The Kallikak Family: A Study in the Heredity of Feeble-Mindedness.* New York: MacMillan, 1912.

Goffman, Irving. *Asylums: Essays on the Social Situation of Mental Patients and Other Inmates.* New York: Doubleday, 1961.

Gold, David. "Beyond the Classroom Walls: Student Writing at Texas Women's University, 1901–1939." *Rhetoric Review* 22, no. 3 (2003): 264–81.

———. *Rhetoric at the Margins: Revising the History of Writing Instruction in American Colleges, 1873–1947.* Carbondale: Southern Illinois University Press, 2008.

Graney, Bernard. *Hervey Backus Wilbur and the Evolution of Policies and Practices Towards Mentally Retarded People.* Dissertation. Syracuse University, 1979.

Hawhee, Debra. *Bodily Arts: Rhetoric and Athletics in Ancient Greece*. Austin: University of Texas Press, 2005.

Houck, Davis, and Amos Kiewe. *FDR's Body Politics: The Rhetoric of Disability*. College Station: Texas A&M University Press, 2003.

Howe, Samuel Gridley. "Memorial to the Legislature of Massachusetts." In *The History of Mental Retardation, Collected Papers*, Vol. 1, edited by M. Rosen, G. Clark, and M. Kivitz. Baltimore: University Park Press, 1976.

"Inspecting an Insane Asylum." *New York Times*. May 11, 1885.

Isocrates. *Antidosis*. Translated by George Norlin. New York: G. P. Putnam, 1928 (Loeb Classical Library).

Itard, Jean-Marc Gaspard. *The Wild Boy of Aveyron*. New York: Appleton, 1962 (1801).

The James Thornton Correspondence, 1855–1866. Syracuse University Special Collections, Bird Library.

Job Books and Samples from Print Shop. New York State Archives, Albany. Cultural Education Department. B1653-99. 1943.

Johnson, Nan. *Nineteenth Century Rhetoric in North America*. Carbondale: Southern Illinois University Press, 1991.

Kates, Susan. *Activist Rhetorics and American Higher Education, 1885–1937*. Carbondale: Southern Illinois University Press, 2001.

Kleege, Georgiana. *Blind Rage: Letters to Helen Keller*. Washington, DC: Gallaudet University Press, 2006.

Lerner, Gerda. *Why History Matters: Life and Thought*. Oxford: Oxford University Press, 1997.

Lewieki-Wilson, Cynthia, and Jay Dolmage. "Refiguring Rhetorica: Linking Feminist Rhetoric and Disability Studies." In *Rhetorica in Motion: Feminist Rhetorical Methods and Methodologies*, edited by E. Schell and K. J. Rawson. Pittsburgh: University of Pittsburgh Press, 2010.

Lewiecki-Wilson, Cynthia, and James Wilson. "Disability, Rhetoric, and the Body." In *Embodied Rhetorics: Disability in Language and Culture*, edited by Lewiecki-Wilson and Wilson. Carbondale: University of Southern Illinois Press, 2001.

Linton, Simi. *Claiming Disability: Knowledge and Identity*. New York, New York University Press, 1998.

Lipson, Carol. "Ancient Egyptian Rhetoric: It All Comes Down to Maat." In *Rhetoric before and beyond the Greeks*, edited by Lipson and Binkley. Albany: State University of New York Press, 2004.

Locke, John. *An Essay Concerning Human Understanding*. Oxford: Clarendon Press, 1975 (1690).

Logan, Shirley Wilson. *Liberating Language: Sites of Rhetorical Education in Nineteenth-Century Black America*. Carbondale: Southern Illinois University Press, 2008.

Longmore, Paul, and Lauri Umansky, eds. *The New Disability History: American Perspectives*. New York: New York University Press, 2001.

Mattingly, Carol. *Appropriating Dress: Women's Rhetorical Style in Nineteenth-Century America*. Carbondale: Southern Illinois University Press, 2002.

———. *Well-tempered Women: Nineteenth Century Temperance Rhetoric*. Carbondale: Southern Illinois University Press, 1998.

McDonagh, Patrick. *"Idiocy": A Cultural History*. Liverpool: Liverpool University Press, 2009.

McDonagh, Patrick and Tim Stainton. *Chasing Shadows: The Historical Construction of Developmental Disability*. *Journal on Developmental Disabilities* 8, no. 2 (Dec 2001): ix–xvi.

McRuer, Robert. "Composing Bodies; or, De-Composition: Queer Theory, Disability Studies, and Alternate Corporealities." *Journal of Advanced Composition* 24 (2004): 47–78.

Mitchell, David, and Sharon Snyder. *Cultural Locations of Disability*. Chicago: University of Chicago Press, 2006.

Mountford, Roxanne. *The Gendered Pulpit: Preaching in American Protestant Spaces*. Carbondale: Southern Illinois University Press, 2003.

Nivison, Kenneth. "'But a Step from College to the Judicial Bench': College and Curriculum in New England's 'Age of Improvement.'" *History of Education Quarterly* 50, no. 4 (Nov. 2010): 460–87.

"Octalog: The Politics of Historiography." *Rhetoric Review* 7, no. 1 (Fall 1988): 5–49.

"Octalog II: The (Continuing) Politics of Historiography." *Rhetoric Review* 16, no. 1. (Autumn 1997): 22–44.

"Octalog III: The Politics of Historiography in 2010." *Rhetoric Review* 30, no. 2 (2011): 109–34.

Onondaga Historical Society. *Syracuse State School—Asylum for Idiots, 1850–1880*.

Ordover, Nancy. *American Eugenics: Race, Queer Anatomy, and the Science of Nationalism*. Minneapolis: University of Minnesota Press, 2003.

"Our State Institutions: Syracuse Past and Present." *New York Times*, November 22, 1871.

Packard, Elizabeth Parsons Ware. "The Prisoner's Hidden Life, or Insane Asylums Unveiled." In *A Mad People's History of Madness*, edited by Dale Peterson. Pittsburgh: University of Pittsburgh Press, 1982.

Padden, Carol, and Tom Humphries. *Inside Deaf Culture*. Cambridge: Harvard University Press, 2005.

Pestalozzi, Johann. "How Gertrude Taught Her Children." In *Significant Contributions to the History of Psychology, 1750–1920*. Ann Arbor: University Publications, 1977 (1801).

Pinel, Philippe. "Treatise on Insanity." In *Significant Contributions to the History of Psychology, 1750–1920*. Ann Arbor: University Publications, 1977 (1806).

Poster, Carol. "Introduction." In *Letter-Writing Manuals and Instruction from Antiquity to the Present*, edited by Poster and Mitchell. Columbia: University of South Carolina Press, 2007.

Price, Margaret. *Mad at School: Rhetorics of Mental Disability and Academic Life*. Ann Arbor: University of Michigan Press, 2011.

Pupil Evaluation Reports. New York State Archives, Albany. Cultural Education Department. B1666., ca. 1860–1909.

Quintilian. *Institutes of Oratory*. http://honeyl.public.iastate.edu/quintilian/index.html.

Rafter, Nicole. *Creating Born Criminals*. Urbana: University of Illinois Press, 1997.

Reaume, Geoffrey. "Portraits of People with Mental Disorders in English Canadian History." *CBMH/BCHM* 17 (2000): 93–125.

Rembis, Michael. "'I Ain't Had Much Schooling': The Ritual of Examination and the Social Construction of Impairment." *Disability Studies Quarterly* 28, no. 3 (Summer, 2008).

Rhetorica ad Herrenium (Ad C. *Herennium de ratione dicendi*). Translated by Harry Caplan. London: Harvard University Press, 1954.

Richards, Penny, and George Sanger. "'To Draw out the Effort of His Mind:' Educating a Child with Mental Retardation in Early-nineteenth Century America." *The Journal of Special Education* 31, no. 4 (Winter 1998): 443–67.

Rose, Martha. *The Staff of Oedipus: Transforming Disability in Ancient Greece*. Ann Arbor: University of Michigan Press, 2003.

Roseboom, William, and Henry Schramm. *They Built a City: Stories and Legends of Syracuse and Onondaga County*. Manlius, NY: Manlius Publishing Co., 1976.

Rothman, David. *Discovery of the Asylum: Social Order and Disorder in the New Republic*. Toronto: Little, Brown, 1971.

Royster, Jacqueline Jones. *Traces of a Stream: Literacy and Social Change Among African American Women*. Pittsburgh: University of Pittsburgh Press, 2000.

———, Gesa Kirsch, and Patricia Bizzell. *Feminist Rhetorical Practices: New Horizons for Rhetoric, Composition, and Literacy Studies*. Carbondale: Southern Illinois University Press, 2012.

Schultz, Lucille. "Pestalozzi's Mark on Nineteenth-Century Composition Instruction: Ideas Not in Words, but in Things." *Rhetoric Review* 14, no. 1 (Autumn 1995): 23–43.

———. *The Young Composers: Composition's Beginnings in Nineteenth-Century Schools*. Carbondale: Southern Illinois University Press, 1999.

Segal, Judy. *Health and the Rhetoric of Medicine*. Carbondale: Southern Illinois University Press, 2008.

Seguin, Edouard. *Idiocy and Its Treatment by the Physiological Method*. New York: Columbia University Teacher's College, 1907 (1866). Web: Disability History Museum, http://www.disabilitymuseum.org/lib/docs/1531.htm; accessed January 15, 2010.

———. "Idiocy as the Effect of Social Evils, and as the Creative Cause of Physiological Education." *The Journal of Psychological Medicine and Diseases of the Nervous System* 4, no. 1: 1–27 (Jan. 10, 1870). Web: Disability History Museum, http://www.disabilitymuseum.org/lib/docs/1581.htm?page=print; accessed January 15, 2010.

———. *Idiocy: Its Diagnosis and Treatment by the Psychological Method*. Translated by L. P. Brockett. Albany: VanBenthuysen's Steam Printing House, 1864.

———. "Institutions for Idiots." *Appletons' Journal* 3 (1870):182–85.

———. "Origin and the Treatment and Training of Idiots." *American Journal of Education* 2 (1856): 145–52. Web: Disability History Museum, http://www.disabilitymuseum.org/lib/docs/1437card.htm; accessed January 15, 2010.

———. "Psycho-Physiological Training of an Idiotic Eye." In *Proceedings of the Association of Medical Officers of American Institutions for Idiotic and Feeble-Minded Persons*. Philadelphia: J. B. Lippincott, 1879.

———. "Psycho-physiological Training of an Idiotic Hand." In *Proceedings of the Association of Medical Officers of American Institutions for Idiotic and Feeble-minded Persons*. Philadelphia: J. B. Lippincott, 1879. Web: Disability History Museum, http://www.disabilitymuseum.org/lib/docs/1908card.htm; accessed November 1, 2009.

The Self-Advocates of Central New York. http://thechp.syr.edu/sacny.htm.

The Self-Advocacy Association of New York State. http://www.sanys.org/index_next.html.

Sheridan, Thomas. *A Course of Lectures on Elocution*. American Archives. http://archive.org/details/acourselectures00shergoog (1803).

Spring, Suzanne B: " 'Seemingly Uncouth Forms': Letters at Mount Holyoke Female Seminary." *College Composition and Communication* 59, no. 4 (June 2008): 633–75.

Stiker, Henri. *A History of Disability*. Ann Arbor: University of Michigan Press, 1997.

"The State Idiot Asylum." *New York Times*, May 19, 1855.

Stuckey, Zosha. "Epideictic Rhetoric and the Reinvention of Disability: A Study of Ceremony at the New York State Asylum for Idiots." *Present Tense: A Journal of Rhetoric in Society* (2012), 2.2. http://www.presenttensejournal.org/volume-2/epideictic-rhetoric-and-the-reinvention-of-disability-a-study-of-the-opening-and-closing-ceremonies-at-the-new-york-state-asylum-for-idiots/.

———. "What Has Become of Jimmy Thornton?: The Rhetoric(s) of Letter-Writing at the New York State Asylum for Idiots, 1855–1866." *Disability Studies Quarterly* 31, no. 3 (2011). http://dsq-sds.org/article/view/1669.

Sutherland, Christine Mason. "Feminist Historiography: Research Methods in Rhetoric." *Rhetoric Society Quarterly* 32, no. 1 (Winter 2002): 109–22.

Syracuse Standard. No title. February 28, 1856.

Talbot, Mabel E. *Edouard Seguin: A Study of an Educational Approach to the Treatment of Mentally Defective Children*. New York: Teachers College at Columbia University, 1964.

Taylor, Steven. *Acts of Conscience: World War II, Mental Institutions, and Religious Objectors*. Syracuse: Syracuse University Press, 2009.

———. "As One Door Closes, Many Open." In *I Can See No Downside to the Closure of the DSO: A Documentary History of the Closure of the Syracuse Developmental Center*, edited by Hall, Mair, Harris, and Lewin. Syracuse: Center on Human Policy Press, 1999.

Tiffany, Francis. *The Life of Dorothea Dix*. Cambridge: Houghton, 1890.

"To His Excellency Governor Hunt." *The Opal*. July 1852. Web: Disability History Museum, http://www.disabilitymuseum.org/lib/docs/1279.htm?page=print; accessed June 1 2010.

Tremain, Shelley. *Foucault and the Government of Disability*. Ann Arbor: University of Michigan Press, 2005.

Trent, James. *Inventing the Feeble-Mind: A History of Mental Retardation in the United States*. Berkeley: University of California Press, 1994.

Vidali, Amy. "Texts of Our Institutional Lives: Performing the Rhetorical Freak Show: Disability, Student Writing, and College Admissions." *College English* 69, no. 6 (July 2008): 615–41.

"Visit of Board of Supervisors to Asylum for Idiots, Almshouse, and Penitentiary," *Syracuse Daily Courier*, January 21, 1858.

Weibezahl, Sue. "Cheers, No Tears, for the Closing of SDC." *The Post-Standard*, June 18, 1998.

Wells, Susan. *Our Bodies, Ourselves, and the Work of Writing*. Palo Alto: Stanford University Press, 2010.

———. *Out of the Dead House: Nineteenth-Century Women Physicians and the Writing of Medicine*. Madison: University of Wisconsin Press, 2001.

Whately, Richard. *Elements of Rhetoric*. 1828. New York: Sheldon, 1871.

White, Hayden. *The Content of Form: Narrative Discourse and Historical Representation*. Baltimore: Johns Hopkins University Press, 1987.

Wilbur, H. B. "The Classifications of 'idiocy.'" In *Proceedings of the Association of Medical Officers of American Institutions for Idiotic and Feeble-minded Persons*. Philadelphia: J. B. Lippincott, 1877. Web: Disaability History Museum, http://www.disabilitymuseum.org/lib/docs/1794card.htm; accessed November 1, 2009.

———. *Governmental Supervision in the Management of the Insane*. Syracuse, New York: unknown, 1876.

———. "Instinct Not Predominant in 'idiocy.'" In *Proceedings of the Association of Medical Officers of American Institutions for Idiotic and Feeble-minded Persons*. Philadelphia: J. B. Lippincott, 1880. Web: http://www.disabilitymuseum.org/lib/docs/1811card.htm; accessed November 1, 2009.

———. "Object System of Instruction as Pursued in the School of Oswego" (Paper presented at the National Teachers Convention at Ogdensburg to the National Association of Teachers). *Barnard's American Journal of Education* 15 (1865) 189–208.

———. "Remarks by Dr. H. B. Wilbur of Syracuse, New York." In *In Memory of Edouard Seguin, M.D.*, supplement to the *Proceedings of the Association of Medical Officers of American Institutions for Idiotic and Feeble-minded Persons*.

———. *Some Suggestions on the Principles and Methods of Elementary Instruction*. 1862. Web: http://quod.lib.umich.edu.libezproxy2.syr.edu/cgi/t/text/text-idx?c=moa;cc=moa;rgn=main;view=text;idno=AJB2126.0001.001.

Winzer, Margaret. *The History of Special Education: From Isolation to Integration*. Washington, DC: Gallaudet University Press, 1993.

Wolfensberger, Wolf. *The Origin and Nature of Our Institutional Models*. Syracuse: Human Policy Press, 1975.

Index

AAMO (American Association for Medical Officers), 49
abolitionism, 18, 20, 25
active life (Seguin)
  reflex life *versus*, 78
  in trinitarian hypothesis, 55–60, 66, 82–83
activist rhetorics (Kates), 98
Acts of Conscience (Taylor), 45
Against the Sophists (Isocrates), 79
Agnew, Lois, 3
almshouses/poorhouses, 7, 19–20, 24, 26, 30, 34–35, 37, 41–48, 79
Amalekites, 31
American Association for Medical Officers (AAMO), 49
American Asylum for Deaf-mutes (Connecticut), 26
American School for the Deaf (Connecticut), 26
Americans with Disabilities Act, 1
  anonymous and nameless trope, 6, 16–17, 40–44, 50, 106
  Aristotle, 94
  art of distributions (Foucault), 32
  Asylums (Goffman), 31–32
asylum-school at Syracuse
anonymous and nameless trope, 6, 16–17, 40–44, 50, 106
archival records on, 6–8, 97–126
asylum-school as term, 24
case histories/pupil evaluation reports, 7–8, 32–43, 105–118, 122–123, 131–132
cognitive dissonance concerning, 17, 100–102, 108–115
curriculum of, 5–7, 10, 127–129 (*see also* Physiological Education [Seguin])
demolitions and closures, 6, 10
described and counted trope, 16–17, 32–40, 115, 124
educational rhetoric and, 4, 5–7, 10, 24–29, 46–50
gymnasium, 58, 63–65, 129
idiot asylums *versus*, 8–9, 29, 32
industrial/occupational education, 10, 27, 29–32, 38–39, 84–90, 127–129
last remaining structure, 6
letter archives, 6–8, 97–126
modes of civic commitments, 3–4
name changes, 24

Americans with Disabilities Act (*continued*)
- nature of, 2–3
- as noble asylum, 16, 17, 18–24, 46–47, 105–108
- opening and dedication (1854), 2–3, 8, 9–10, 16–17, 19–23, 57, 125
- origins in Albany (1851–1854), 9–10, 20, 23–24, 35, 38, 46–48, 57, 88–89, 104, 117–118
- phusiopoesis and, 4, 13, 54, 94
- Physiological Education of special education (*see* Physiological Education [Seguin])
- prison role, 16, 24, 26–32
- rehabilitation and, 5–6, 16, 27–29
- reporting techniques, 7–8, 32–43
- resident council/patient advisory board, 10, 125
- runaways, 29, 30, 131–132
- school role, 4, 5–7, 10, 16, 24–29, 46–50
- selection and admission process, 2–3, 17, 34–36, 39, 87, 118
- size and growth, 6, 8–9, 10, 23, 24, 38, 46, 87–91, 106
- Syracuse University *versus*, 128–130, 134–135
- visited and displayed trope, 16–17, 44–50, 116–123

Atwood, Margaret, 53
audiological moment (Brueggemann), 4

Backboard, 64
Backus, Frederick, 20, 22, 23–24
Baynton, Douglas, 95, 129, 133, 140n5
Beers, Clifford, 124
Bell, A. G., 140n5
benevolence, 16, 21, 80–81, 105–108
Bentham, Jeremy, 29
Berkenkotter, Carol, 41
Berlin, James, 99
Berube, Michael, 17
Bicêtre, The School For Deaf Mutes (Paris), 55, 59, 80, 84
Biklen, Douglas, 11, 131
Binet, Alfred, 2, 34, 137–138n4
biopower (Foucault), 30, 31, 32
Birth of the Clinic (Foucault), 50
Bogdan, Robert, 48
Bonet, Juan Pablo, 60
Brueggemann, Brenda, 2, 4, 95, 129, 134, 140n5
bureaucratic rhetoric, 97–126
- case histories/pupil evaluation reports, 7–8, 32–43, 105–118, 122–123, 131–132
- cognitive dissonance concerning, 17, 100–102, 108–115
- competing forces and actions in, 98
- *James Thornton Correspondence, The*, 7, 98, 101, 102–116, 117, 119, 120
- letters of family members *versus*, 101–102, 116–123
- overview of letters, 101–102
- petitions of families, 101, 102, 103, 117–118
- power dynamics, 102, 115–123
- rhetoric of participation, 98–100

Byrom, Brad, 27, 133

Campbell, George, 78, 93
capital punishment, 125
Carlson, Elof Axel, 31
case histories/pupil evaluation reports, 7–8, 32–43, 105–118, 122–123, 131–132
Center on Human Policy, 10
Charland, Louis C., 80
Cicero, Marcus Tullius, 3, 4, 72–73, 132–133, 138n5
civic participation, 3–4, 56, 82–83, 93–95, 135
civil rights advocacy, 10, 24
Civil War, 23
Claiming Disability (Linton), 54
Clerc, Laurent, 26, 140n5
Cobb, Amanda J., 2, 28, 76
cognitive dissonance, 17, 100–102, 108–115
Collins (Tolar Burton), Vicki, 100–101, 130–131

common school movement, 9, 25–26, 27, 76–77, 104–105
compulsory public education, 26–27
Condillac, Étienne de, 28, 56, 58–59, 62, 66–67
Connecticut Idiot Asylum, 48–49
Connors, Robert, 74
conscientious objectors, 45
Corbett, Edward, 58–59, 92
Crowley, Sharon, 68
Cuff, John, 43
Cultural Locations of Disability (Mitchell and Snyder), 27, 133–134

Danvers State Hospital (Massachusetts), 6
Darby, Penney, 6
de Certeau, Michel, 101
deficit approach, 134–135
Demosthenes, 4, 75, 138n6
Derrida, Jacques, 101
Descartes, René, 67
described and counted trope, 16–17, 32–40, 115, 124
Dewey, John, 53
disability
  alliance with feminist studies, 12
  biopower (Foucault) and, 30, 31, 32
  categories in census, 36–37, 115
  deficit approach, 134–135
  disability rights movement, 1–2, 10, 137n1
  "feeble-minded" as term, 2, 9, 27, 137n3
  "idiot" as term, 2, 4, 9, 11, 16, 33–40, 50–51, 137n2
  Other and, 11, 17
  rhetoric and disability studies, 1–3, 10–12, 48, 123–126, 133–134
Discipline and Punish (Foucault), 31
Discovery of the Asylum (Rothman), 18
Dix, Dorothea, 23, 44–46, 139n12
Dolmage, Jay, 2, 134, 139n9
Doren, G. A., 90
drawing instruction, 73–74
DuBois, W. E. B., 127
Duffy, John, 2, 99
Dunn, Patricia Ann, 2

education
  purpose of, 93–94
  rhetoric and, 4, 5–7, 10, 16, 24–29, 46–50 (*see also* Physiological Education [Seguin])
Education for All Handicapped Children Act (EHA), 27, 91
Edwards, R. A. R., 105, 140nn5–6
efficio, 35
Einhorn, Lois J., 1
Elgin State Hospital (Illinois), 6
Ellis Island, 9, 139n9
elopement, 29, 30, 131–132
England, 19, 28, 60, 80
Enlightenment, 18, 25–26, 55
Enoch, Jessica, 2
epideictic/sentimental rhetoric, 16, 22–23, 30, 139n3
Erie Canal, 5, 19–20, 86, 107, 128
Ervelles, Nirmala, 12
Esquirol, Jean-Étienne Dominique, 55
ethopoeia, 35
etiquette, 81–82, 83
eugenics movement, 43–44, 88–90
Extraordinary Bodies (Garland-Thomson), 17

face and countenance, 64, 65, 79–80
Fahnestock, Jeanne, 18
Fairmont Farm, 84–85
farming, 84–85
feeble-minded
  applied to immigrants, 9, 139n9
  desire to eradicate, 90
  as term, 2, 9, 27, 137n3
feminist studies, 12, 18, 20, 25, 138n11, 139n6
Ferguson, Philip, 101, 116
Fletcher-Janzen, Elaine, 2–3, 27, 34
Foucault, Michel, 30–31, 32, 50
France, 25–26, 28, 30–31, 55, 59, 80–81, 84, 130
Franklin, Benjamin, 82

Fredal, James, 134
French Enlightenment, 25–26
Frost, John, 74
Fuller, Elmer E., 43
Fuller, Emma E., 43
functional circle (Seguin), 66–67

Gallaudet, Thomas Hopkins, 26, 140n5
garden-system, 63
Garland-Thomson, Rosemarie, 11, 12, 17
Geertz, Clifford, 132
gendered rhetoric, 38–39
Germany, 25
Glenn, Cheryl, 4, 12, 99, 125, 131, 132, 138n7, 141nn4–5
Goddard, Henry, 9, 27, 43–44, 88, 137–138n4
Goffman, Erving, 30, 31–32, 40, 42, 50, 125, 138n15, 141
Gold, David, 2, 28, 68, 76, 94, 98, 99, 133
Graney, Bernard, 57
Gray, R. H., 104–106
Great Britain, 19, 25, 28, 60, 80
Great Confinement, 31
group homes, 10

hand, in education process, 61–63, 75
hidden curriculum (Cobb), 28
high school, 26
HIPAA (Health Insurance Portability and Accountability Act), 41
History of Disability, A (Stiker), 27–28
History of Special Education, The (Winzer), 26–27
hospital-school (Byrom), 27
Houck, Davis W., 1
Howe, Julia Ward, 138n11, 139n6
Howe, Samuel Gridley, 9–10, 16, 20, 25, 26, 27, 57, 138n11, 139n6, 140n5
Howe, Wilbur, 16
How Gertrude Taught Her Children (Pestalozzi), 60
human rights violations, 24
Hunt, Washington, 15, 21, 34, 125, 138n12
Hutchinson, L., 102–103, 111, 112
Hygiene and Education (Seguin), 66

identity kit (Goffman), 32, 42
ideology of extinction (Mitchell and Snyder), 6
idiocy
  applied to immigrants, 9, 139n9
  desire to eradicate, 90
  disability as deficit and, 134–135
  enumeration in census, 36–37, 115
  gaze in situating, 16–17, 44–50
  madness/insanity *versus*, 30–31, 36
  as metonymic state (McDonagh), 18
  progressive educational reform and, 20, 21–22, 24–29, 54–57
  rehabilitation focus and, 5–6, 16, 27–29
  situation within rhetorical modes, 17
  social and rhetorical construction, 17, 23
  as term, 2, 4, 9, 11, 16, 33–40, 50–51, 137n2
  Hervey Backus Wilbur concept of, 33–40, 51
Idiocy (McDonagh), 17
Idiocy: Its Treatment by the Physiological Method (Seguin), 57
idiot asylums, 8–9, 29, 32
Illinois Mental Asylum (Jacksonville), 124
imitation
  personal *versus* objective, 67–68
  rote practice *versus*, 60–62, 67–68, 76
  as social relation, 67–69, 72, 74–77
immigrant population
  idiocy/feeble-mindedness of, 9, 139n9
  increase in, 23
inclusive education, 138n14, 139–140n2
"incurables," 87–90
individual rights, 25
Individuals with Disabilities Education Act (IDEA), 27, 91

industrial/occupational education, 10, 27, 29–32, 38–39, 84–90, 127–129
inmates, as term, 88
inscription of action (Geertz), 132
institutionalization, 29–32
  noble asylum, 18–24, 46–47, 105–108
intellectual disabled, 2
intelligence, 2–3, 9, 27, 34, 35, 36, 88, 137–138n4
Inventing the Feeble-Mind (Trent), 48
IQ tests, 2–3, 9, 27, 34, 35, 36, 88, 137–138n4
Isocrates, 72, 79, 94
Itard, Jean-Marc Gaspard, 28, 55, 56, 59–60, 66–67, 84, 130

James Thornton Correspondence, The, 7, 98, 101, 102–116, 117, 119, 120
Johnson, Nan, 76

Kallikak Family, The (Goddard), 43–44
Kates, Susan, 98, 99
Keller, Helen, 1, 2, 16, 25, 57, 138n11
Kiewe, Amos, 1
Kitzhaber, Albert, 74
Kliewer, Christopher, 131
Knight, Henry, 48–49

language instruction, 71–73, 92–93
laundry, 86–87, 88
Leavenworth, Elias W., 21, 138n12
Lewiecki-Wilson, Cynthia, 2
Life as We Know It (Berube), 17
Linton, Simi, 54
Lipson, Carol, 102, 117
listening skills, 70–71, 74–75
literate disconnection, 130–132
Lives They Left Behind, The (Darby and Stastny), 6
Locke, John, 56, 58–59, 62, 66–67, 92
Logan, Shirley Wilson, 2, 143n2
Longmore, Paul, 5, 11
Lowell, Josephine Shaw, 141n10

Madness and Civilization (Foucault), 30–31
Mann, Horace, 9–10, 25, 26, 140n5
masculinity, 38–39
Massachusetts Asylum for the Blind, 25–27
Mayo, Elizabeth, 74
May, Samuel J., 15, 21, 26, 54–55, 139n7, 140n3
McDonagh, Patrick, 17, 18
medical rhetoric, 39–40, 105–106, 122–123, 133–134
memotechny (Seguin), 68
mental illness, 30–31, 36, 80–81, 124
Methodical Memory, The (Crowley), 68
military service, 38, 65, 86
Mind That Found Itself, A (Beers), 124
Mitchell, David, 6, 27, 133–134
Monroe, Allen, 21, 138n12
Monroe County Poorhouse, 43
Montessori, Maria, 28, 56, 74
moral treatment, 28, 55–57, 78–83, 86–87
Morgan, Christopher, 139n4
Mount Holyoke Female Seminary, 102
Mulford, E. F., 106–109, 111–112, 142n16
musical instruction, 69–71, 77

Nameless One, 40
National Institution for Deaf-Mutes (France), 28
Native American education, 28
New Disability History, The (Longmore and Umansky), 11
New Paltz County House, 131
New York Central Railroad, 107
New York City
  asylums in, 10, 55, 72, 82
  disability rights movement, 1–2, 10, 137n1
New York Institution for Deaf and Dumb, 26
New York State Archives, 6–7, 97–126
New York State Asylum for Idiots (Syracuse), 2–3. *See also* asylum-school at Syracuse

New York State Insane Asylum (Utica), 124
New York State School for the Deaf (Rome), 104, 115
Nietzsche, Frederick, 101
noble asylum role, 16, 17, 18–24, 46–47, 105–108
notions, 66–67

Oakwood Cemetery, Syracuse, 6
object method, 60–63, 76–77
occupational/industrial training, 10, 27, 29–32, 38–39, 84–90, 127–129
Onondaga County Poorhouse (Syracuse), 45
Onondaga Historical Society, 6
Oralism, 69, 142n11
oral method, of teaching deaf, 60, 140n5
order, 79–81
Ordover, Nancy, 9
Origin and Nature of Our Institutional Models, The (Wolfensberger), 88
orphanages, 23–24, 48
Oswego System of Object Instruction, 61–63
Other, disability and, 11, 17
Out of the Dead House (Wells), 131

Packard, Elizabeth Parsons Ware, 124
Paine, Thomas, 82
Pan American Exposition (Buffalo), 76, 98, 117, 122–123
Paris Asylum for the Insane and Idiotic, 80
parole, 125
patients rights movement, 10
Patient Tales (Berkenkotter), 41
pedagogy of association (Seguin), 69
Pennsylvania Training School, 49
Pereire, Jacob Rodriguez, 56, 60, 69
Perkins Institute/School for the Blind (Massachusetts), 25–27, 138n11
Pestalozzi, Johann, 28, 56, 60–61, 68
Philosophy of Rhetoric (Campbell), 93
phusiopoesis, 4, 13, 54, 94
Physiological Education (Seguin), 21–22, 34, 53–95
- application in asylum-school, 56–57
- drawing instruction, 73–74
- face and countenance, 64, 65, 79–80
- garden-system, 63
- hand in, 61–63, 75
- imitation as social relation, 67–69, 72, 74–77
- "incurables," 87–90
- integration into civic participation, 56, 82–83, 93–95
- language instruction, 71–73, 92–93
- listening, 70–71, 74–75
- moral treatment, 28, 55–57, 78–83, 86–87
- musical instruction, 69–71, 77
- notions, 66–67
- object method, 60–63, 76–77
- occupational training, 84–90
- order in, 79–81
- posture, 64–65
- reading instruction, 75–77
- roots of "special" education and, 54–57
- sensation as entry-point for learning, 56, 57–60, 62–64, 66–67, 91–92
- social decorum and etiquette in, 79–82, 83
- speech instruction, 69–73, 77, 92–93
- trinitarian hypothesis, 55–60, 66, 82–83
- unintended consequences of, 95
- walking, 64–65, 92
- will in, 78–82
- writing instruction, 61, 74–76, 77, 92

Pinel, Philippe, 28, 55, 80–81
poorhouses/almshouses, 7, 19–20, 24, 26, 30, 34–35, 37, 41–48, 79
Poster, Carol, 102, 117, 141n9
posture, 64–65
power dynamics, 12, 31, 99, 102, 115–123
Price, Margaret, 2
prison role of asylum, 16, 24, 26–32

privacy rights, 41
progressive educational reform, 9, 16, 19–22, 24, 25–26, 54–57, 68, 91, 128
public education, 18, 24. *See also* asylum-school at Syracuse
  common school movement, 9, 25–26, 27, 76–77, 104–105
  compulsory, 26–27

Quintilian, 75, 132–133

Randall's Island Asylum (New York), 55, 72, 82
reading instruction, 75–77, 104, 112
reflective processes, 77, 78, 93
rehabilitation focus, 5–6, 16, 27–29
Rembis, Michael, 131
restraints, 80–81
rhetoric
  access and, 3, 4
  anonymous and nameless trope, 6, 16–17, 40–44, 50, 106
  asylum as prison, 16, 24, 26–32
  asylum as school, 4, 5–7, 10, 16, 24–29, 46–50
  of bureaucratic letter writing (*see* bureaucratic rhetoric)
  of case histories/pupil evaluation reports, 7–8, 32–43, 105–118, 122–123, 131–132
  civic participation and, 3–4, 56, 82–83, 93–95, 135
  complex meaning of, 3–4, 5–7, 10, 99
  described and counted trope, 16–17, 32–40, 115, 124
  development of rhetorical history, 6–7
  disability culture and, 1–3, 10–12, 48, 123–126, 133–134
  education and, 4, 5–7, 10, 16, 24–29, 46–50 (*see also* Physiological Education [Seguin])
  effictio, 35
  emergence of field, 10
  epideictic/sentimental, 16, 22–23, 30, 139n3
  ethopoeia, 35
  gendered, 38–39
  medical, 39–40, 105–106, 122–123, 133–134
  methods of analysis, 11–12, 35
  of noble asylum, 16, 17, 18–24, 46–47, 105–108
  participation and, 98–100, 129
  presence and, 3, 23, 129, 130–132
  of remnants, 1–3, 5–7, 123–126, 129–132
  rhetorical accretion (Collins), 100–101, 130–131
  of silence, 5, 6, 13, 98–100, 116, 124–126, 129, 132
  topoi (topics), 13, 16
  tropes (figures) (*see* tropes [figures])
  in urge to improve and transform, 4, 13, 54, 94
  visitations and, 16–17, 44–50, 116–123
Rhetorical Figures in Science (Fahnestock), 18
Rhetoric at the Margins (Gold), 98
Rochester Poorhouse, 43
Rome State Custodial Asylum (New York), 6, 104
Roosevelt, Franklin D., 1
Roseboom, William, 26
Rose, Martha, 138n6
rote memorization, 60–62, 67–68, 76
Rothman, David, 18
Royal Society of London, 60
Royster, Jacqueline Jones, 2, 100, 141n6
runaways, 29, 30, 131–132
Russ, John, 26

savants, 70
Saville, H. H., 107–108, 111, 142n14, 142n16
Schultz, Lucille, 61, 68, 74, 76–77
Seguin, Edouard, 6, 16, 21–22, 26, 28, 34, 53–95, 128, 129–130, 133, 135

self-advocacy movement, 10, 142–143n19
self-regulation, 72
Sensation Room, 58, 62–64
sewing, 85–87, 88
Shaw, Robert Gould, 141n10
sheltered workshop approach, 10, 27, 29–32, 38–39, 84–90, 127–129
Sheridan, Thomas, 132–133
Ship of Fools (Foucault), 30
sign language, 1, 60, 69, 104, 105, 112, 140n6, 142n11, 142n13
silence, rhetoric and, 5, 6, 13, 98–100, 116, 124–126, 129, 132
Snyder, Sharon, 6, 27, 133–134
Snyder, Willis, 43
social constructivist theory, 11, 17
social decorum, 79–82, 83
Sophists, 65–66, 79
Spain, 80, 140n4
special education, 24, 27. *See also* Physiological Education (Seguin)
  general education *versus*, 53–54, 94
  inclusive education *versus*, 138n14, 139–140n2
  roots of, 54–57
speech instruction, 69–73, 77, 92–93
Spenser, Herbert, 67
Spring, Suzanne B., 102
Stastny, Peter, 6
stealing, 82
Steuben County Board of Supervisors, 115
Stiker, Henri, 5, 27–28
Stoics, 93
Switzerland, 25
Syracuse Asylum for Idiots. *See* asylum-school at Syracuse
Syracuse Board of Education, 26
Syracuse Developmental Center, 10
Syracuse State Institution for Feeble-Minded Children/Syracuse State School. *See* asylum-school at Syracuse
Syracuse University, 48, 103, 128–130, 134–135
tabula rasa (Locke), 58–59, 66
Talbot, Mabel E., 55, 56, 57, 59, 63
Taylor, Steven J., 11, 45
temperance, 18
Texas Women's University, 94
Thornton, James, 130
  James Thornton Correspondence, The, 7, 98, 101, 102–116, 117, 119, 120
  timeline, 103–104
Thornton, Richard H., 105
Thornton/Whead, Mary, 98, 101, 102–116, 117, 119, 120, 130
Tiffany, Francis, 44
Tilyon, Cora, 43
Tompkins County Poorhouse, 43
topoi (topics), 13, 16
total institution (Goffman), 30, 31–32, 40, 50
Traces of a Stream (Royster), 100
Traitment Moral (Seguin), 57
Treatise on Insanity (Pinel), 80–81
Treatise on Sensations (Condillac), 59
Tremain, Shelley, 31
Trent, James, 11, 23, 48, 55, 57, 66
trinitarian hypothesis (Seguin), 55–60, 66, 82–83
tropes (figures), 13, 16–17, 51
  anonymous and nameless, 6, 16–17, 40–44, 50, 106
  asylum as noble, 16, 17, 18–24, 46–47, 105–108
  asylum as prison, 16, 24, 26–32
  asylum as school, 4, 5–7, 10, 16, 24–29, 46–50
  described and counted, 16–17, 32–40, 115, 124
  in transference of meaning, 18
  visited and displayed, 16–17, 44–50, 116–123
Tuke, William, 19, 28, 80

Umansky, Lauri, 5, 11
Underground Railroad, 20
Unfit, The (Carlson), 31
universal education, 25, 142n13

Unspoken (Glenn), 99

Victor, Wild Boy of Aveyron, 28, 55, 56, 59, 84, 130
Vidali, Amy, 2
Vineyard Training School (New Jersey), 44
Virginia School for Deaf, 26
visited and displayed trope, 16–17, 44–50, 116–123

walking, 64–65, 92
Washington, Booker T., 127
Weld, L. L., 102–103
Wells, Susan, 131
Whately, Richard, 72
Whead, Thomas, 105, 115
White, Hayden, 101
Wilbur, Harriet H., 112–113, 120
Wilbur, Hervey Backus
  bureaucratic rhetoric and, 98, 102–111, 114–119
  curriculum of asylum-school (*see* Physiological Education [Seguin])
  custodial and industrial goals and, 27, 29–32, 38–39, 84–90, 127–129
  death in 1883, 89–91
  defining idiocy, 33–40, 51
  education goals and, 24–29, 46–50
  letters to Mrs. Thornton, 7, 98, 101, 102–116, 117, 119, 120
  opening of New York State Asylum for Idiots (Syracuse), 2–3, 8, 9–10, 16–17, 19–23, 57, 125
  private school in Barre, Massachusetts, 26–27, 57
  reporting techniques, 32–43
  as Superintendent of asylum-school, 6, 9–10, 21–29
  visitations and, 45–50
Wild Boy of Aveyron, 28, 55, 56, 59, 84, 130
will, 78–82
Willard State Hospital (New York), 6, 115
Willowbrook Institution (New York), 10
Wilson, Cynthia Lewieki, 11
Wilson, James C., 11
Winzer, Margaret, 26–27, 140n4
Wolfensberger, Wolf, 88
women's rights, 12, 18, 20, 25, 138n11, 139n6
Worcester State Hospital (Massachusetts), 6
World War II, 45
writing instruction, 61, 74–76, 77, 92, 104, 105, 112, 120, 123

York Retreat for Idiots and the Insane (England), 19, 28, 80
Young Composers, The (Schultz), 61